The Tide Always Comes Back

To Keith with
warm regards

Carnale
2014

Also by Jean Carnahan

If Walls Could Talk

Don't Let the Fire Go Out!

The Tide Always Comes Back

and Other Irrefutable Truths and Assurances

Senator Jean Carnahan

SKYHORSE PUBLISHING

Skyhorse Publishing books may be purchased in bulk at special discounts for sales promotion, corporate gifts, fund-raising, or educational purposes. Special editions can also be created to specifications. For details, contact the Special Sales Department, Skyhorse Publishing, 555 Eighth Avenue, Suite 903, New York, NY 10018 or info@skyhorsepublishing.com.

www.skyhorsepublishing.com

10 9 8 7 6 5 4 3 2 1

Library of Congress Cataloging-in-Publication Data
Carnahan, Jean.
The tide always comes back, and other irrefutable truths and assurances / Senator Jean Carnahan.
p. cm.
ISBN 978-1-60239-744-6 (hardcover : alk. paper)
1. Carnahan, Jean. 2. Carnahan, Jean.--Philosophy. 3. Legislators--United States--Biography. 4. Women legislators--United States--Biography. 5. United States. Congress. Senate--Biography. I. Title.
E840.8.C365A3 2009
328.73'092--dc22
[B]
2009014215

Printed in the United States of America

For my grandsons Austin and Andrew and
my granddaughters Sydney and Harper:

"If ever there is a tomorrow when we're not together,
there is something you must always remember:
You are braver than you believe, stronger than you seem,
and smarter than you think.
But the most important thing is,
even if we're apart, I'll always be with you."
—*Winnie the Pooh*

Contents

Introduction

Family. Faith. Freedom. I took these three wonderful gifts for granted until they were all endangered by a tragic and incredible convergence of events at the turn of the century. In 2000, my husband, Governor Mel Carnahan, and Senator John Ashcroft were locked in an epic battle for the U. S. Senate seat in Missouri. Within three weeks of the general election, the plane carrying my husband, my oldest son, and a long-time staffer crashed into a wooded hillside near St. Louis. All three were killed instantly. When my husband was elected posthumously, I took his place in the U. S. Senate during one of the most troubled times in our nation's history.

More misfortune was to come eleven months later. My farmhouse, which I had called home for twenty-seven years, was struck by lightning and burned. Two days after that, as I sorted through the rubble, I received word that our country had been attacked by terrorists. Pieces of the airplane that struck the Pentagon had floated down onto my car parked in Pentagon City.

After the 9/11 attacks, Capitol Hill was more like Bunker Hill as we geared up for whatever might come next. Like every other senator, I now had a government-issued gas mask in my desk drawer, and I knew the "secret" place to assemble should we be forced to evacuate the Capitol quickly.

During the weeks following the anthrax mailings to my Senate office building, I found out more about chemical and biological agents than I wanted to know. When we were displaced during the two-month clean up, it took a heap of patience and a touch of humor to operate an office scattered over three locations. The heightened security, the bomb scares, and the evacuations added yet another layer of anxiety on top of the hectic senatorial and campaign schedules. In the midst of all the chaos, my own sadness melded with that of our nation.

I was taught to believe that all our wounds and woes come with blessings attached; that uncovering the blessing is part of the healing. In my search, I found solace in some enduring and irrefutable truths, such as the old Cornish proverb I use as the title of this book. I adopt other truths for chapter titles, as I reflect on such topics as childhood, tradition, values, memories, encouragement, loss, forgiveness, faith, language, doubt, marriage, change, aging, liberty, questioning, family secrets, grief, optimism, patience, poverty, patriotism, and the future.

Writing these homilies has been an extraordinary, heartwarming adventure. Oftentimes my thoughts bubbled up like spring water and spilled onto the page amid falling tears. Other times my impish Muse would come up with a sentence of Shakespearean quality when, unfortunately, I was in the checkout line at the supermarket or drifting into the twilight zone late at night.

There's something about soaking in a steamy, hot bath that causes words to ooze from my pores. I keep a pencil near, but too often no paper. I have discovered that the Italian tiles surrounding my tub make a perfect "chalk board" for a phrase I want to preserve. The words of the prophets may be written on the subway wall, but mine are scrawled on the bathroom wall. I try to transcribe them before the cleaning woman arrives. She and Mr. Clean once removed my outline for an entire chapter with a single stroke.

Still, I was not to be deterred. Samuel Johnson said, "A man will turn over half a library to make a book." I contend that a woman will turn over a *whole* library, scour a hard drive, and unsettle a household, or two, in order to write a book.

Writing about family caused such intense reverie that I was frequently sidetracked by urges to hunt down lost relatives, label old photos, or force my grandkids to listen to tales of my youth. When I wrote of faith, I voiced the enduring beliefs that have sustained me during times of disaster and heartbreak. The chapters on freedom allowed me to do a little flag waving, which is permitted to those in my age bracket. I questioned our leaders, expressed my political allegiance to the Democratic Party, and relived those years during World War II when patriotism was our common virtue.

When books are written, the blame must be placed somewhere. That's where children come in handy. I place the blame for my writing this book squarely on my family. After I finished my autobiography *Don't Let the Fire Go Out*, published in 2004, they urged me to write more. Perhaps that was to help me endure my knee and hip surgeries and to overcome the other indignities of aging.

I wish I could tell you that I'm an expert in something, but I am not. Over the past seventy-five years, I have been a mother, politician's wife, First Lady, U. S. Senator, avid reader, writer, blogger, speaker, and traveler. I speak but one language and muddle through a couple of others, as needed. I am a wellspring of trivia and random verse, a generalist, adhering to Blaise Pascal's notion that "since we cannot know all there is to be known about anything, we ought to know a little about everything." In that spirit, I reminisce, I hope, I encourage, I dream, I discover, I laugh, I question, I advise and . . . most of all, I believe.

For those of you looking at the title of this book and thinking you were buying a treatise on oceanography, my apologies. This book is about certainty—where to find it and how to enjoy it.

Jean Carnahan

St. Louis, Missouri

2009

Foreword

My mother was "cursed"—as she puts it—with the creative gene in the family. She bubbles with ideas, loves to play with words, and amuses family and audiences with her self-effacing humor and storytelling. I often call her when I need an illustration to make a point, knowing that she has a fifty-year collection of anecdotes, opening lines, and jokes.

When I'm lucky, she'll e-mail me an assortment to chose from; other times she replies, "Sorry, the well's dry, but I'll keep digging."

When I first ran for public office, she told me the secret of giving a good speech. "Follow the advice of Liz Carpenter and you'll never go wrong," she said.

"You mean Aunt Lizzy Carpenter?" I asked, knowing that I had a great-aunt by that name.

"No, I mean the Liz Carpenter who was the press secretary for Lady Bird Johnson and an extremely witty woman. Liz said, 'Put the laugh at the beginning, the meat in the middle, and raise the flag at the end.'"

Good advice. I've watched Mom do that time and again, though she mostly attributes her ability to move audiences (and readers) to having observed so many preachers from the pew of a Baptist church when she was a child. But my grandfather shared the knack for storytelling, too, knowing intuitively how to deliver a punch line with maximum impact.

When I first read this manuscript, I found my mother's words had a delightful familiarity. I've heard her tell the stories; I've witnessed many of the events she describes and shared the feelings that she unveils.

I also found assurance in the title she chose: *The Tide Always Comes Back*. Life is like the returning tide, its tow pulling us farther into the deep than we wish to go, delivering us onto "undreamed shores." I can see why my mother is so attracted to the tide; it is a symbol of struggle, endurance, and renewal. The tide never gives up—nor does she.

Robin Carnahan

Missouri Secretary of State

2009

The Tide Always Comes Back

Family

Families are like old quilts. Although they tend to unravel at times, each can be stitched back together with love.

—Unknown

Change Is Gonna Come

Change comes like a little wind that ruffles the curtains at dawn and it comes like the stealthy perfume of wildflowers hidden in the grass.

—John Steinbeck

It's been said that the only people who like change are busy cashiers and wet babies. Yet change is occurring all around—and within—us, whether we like it or not. Change is unfair, inconvenient, and inevitable. Like ambient light, it comes at us from all directions. As Steinbeck implies in the earlier quotation, change can be a sneaky rascal coming out of nowhere, slowly engulfing us; sometimes tripping us up.

In preparation for whatever might come, I try to remain nimble of mind and body. Recently, I made a preemptive strike on some old habits long in need of correction. It is good to make changes of our choosing, knowing there'll be a God's plenty of those we don't choose. Uprooting my old ways was not meant to be a spiritual venture—though it has that potential. I just wanted to get rid of some things that no longer worked for me.

I undertook the task with Spartan resolve, knowing that any attempt to mend my ways would not be easy. Here's what I did:

I no longer keep the plastic bag of extra buttons that come attached to a newly purchased garment. I reclaimed an entire dresser drawer when I bravely trashed my decades-old collection.

I got rid of scented candles, too, keeping only one formed from a lovely pressed glass jar, a gift from my departed friend, Sonia. Like our long friendship, it has many facets.

I quit giving advice to my kids, not because they don't need it, but because it makes me feel senile when they smile pleasantly, pat me on the hand, and say, "Thank you for sharing that with me." From now on, I will concentrate on my grandkids. They have never lived with me or been exposed to my many faults and thus find me incredibly loveable.

I no longer taunt myself with the clothes in the back of my closet that will never fit again. As Popeye often said, "I yam what I yam." Well, I yam never going to be a size 10 again.

I quit feeling bad about unfiled recipes, unsorted photographs, and an untidy hard drive. I am able to find most things most of the time or at least, some things some of the time.

I no longer feel bad for not watching all the Netflix movies that I excitedly picked out six months ago, including the documentary on the history of the oil industry.

I am no longer bothered by towels and wash cloths that don't match. Same for pots, dishes, and glassware.

I'm not polishing silver anymore. Anything that requires more care and cleaning than the family pet goes to the attic or up on eBay.

I'm discarding my moderate but irrational fear of long elevator rides. I was only stuck once in my life, in Rome, in an overloaded cage elevator. I am thinking about taking up a new fear that holds more promise of occurring, like a fear of more losses in my 401(k) account.

I got rid of all my magazines that are over a year old and began giving away books, since the shelves, night tables, and corners of my rooms reached capacity and my walk space was narrowing.

I feel relief at having extracted some of the clutter and triviality from my life. They're small steps, but I feel better already.

Embracers Versus Resistors

While we can make personal changes at our leisure, technological change is less under our control. When it comes to innovation, we are either Embracers or Resistors. (You might include the Tolerators, but they're a wishy-washy group, so I will let them be.) Embracers don't wait for life or technology to overtake them. They stay out front ready to welcome new methods, new people, and new experiences—everything from hi-tech gadgetry to stray dogs. These people are excited by life and expectations of the future. They want to know more, see more, be more.

Resistors are cautious, risk-averse, and slow to adapt. They find change discomforting. While the Embracers are thinking things could get better; the Resistors are fearful that things could get worse. If life were a fast-moving locomotive, they are the throttle throwers, seeing danger around every curve. Embracers, on the other hand, are fueling the engine to create the power to take on the next hill. Historically, Resistors have met with only limited success, but they continue to put up a valiant struggle to slow things down.

It's hard to imagine that there was once strong resistance to some of the conveniences we have come to accept. When the dial telephone was first introduced by the Bell System in the 1920s, people didn't like having to place phone calls themselves without the assistance of an operator. Ma Bell had to engage in a massive public relations program to persuade users that rotary dialing was superior to dealing with a switchboard operator. Not everyone was convinced. One U. S. Senator was so distraught by the new system that he introduced a bill calling for the removal of dial phones from congressional offices. Finally, a compromise was reached that allowed lawmakers to choose which device they preferred.

The Speed of Change

Even those who are excited by innovation find it hard to keep up with the pace of change. Until the 20th century, humanity was fairly sluggish in its development. When you compare our progress during that century with previous eras, you can see how busy we've been.

Human beings have been on this planet for some eight hundred generations. We've had recorded history during the last seventy; the printed page only during the last six. In the past two generations, we developed the electric motor, light bulb, automobile, and radio. During my lifetime, innovation has skyrocketed, bringing us such marvels as radar, television, penicillin, jet planes, satellites, microwaves, heart pacemakers, nuclear power, the computer, and the Internet—to name a few. *There have been greater breakthroughs in the last one hundred years than in all of the previous history of mankind.*

The pace is not likely to slacken. Nor will today's knowledge be adequate for tomorrow. As futurist Alvin Toffler warned, we must be willing "to learn, unlearn, and relearn." Those who adapt to this new paradigm will thrive; those who don't will fall behind. That's the way it's always been.

A Peek into the Future

My first look at the future came with a trip to New York for the 1939–1940 World's Fair. In those halcyon pre-war days, my parents were awed by futuristic transportation, the first television, and punched cards on which data could be sorted and read. At age seven, my regret was missing an earlier appearance of Superman, the idol of every American kid.

Twenty-five years later, I visited another World's Fair, again in New York. This time, I stood in line to view an intriguing new contraption. Fairgoers were allowed to test one of its many capabilities. By typing in your birth date, it would display your exact age to the day.

The man in front of me was skeptical. He decided to outwit the device by giving less information than requested. Attempting to defy technology, he entered only the last two digits of his birth year. With a smirk on his face, he folded his arms, rocked back on his heels, and waited defiantly. His wife gasped and covered her mouth with her hand.

Then she tugged at his arm, as if expecting some form of retribution to come upon them if they stood too near.

But, the machine sounded no alarm. No smoke belched from its innards. The clever invention simply flashed his age upon the screen calculated to the year (rather than the day) and bid him a courteous, "Thank you for coming to the fair."

After that, those in line stood respectfully silent, taking their turn watching the mechanical wizard answer correctly every time. None of us had any idea what a transforming effect this entertaining novelty would someday have upon our lives.

"How much does it cost?" I inquired.

"Twenty thousand dollars," someone said.

Well, there won't be many around at those prices, I thought to myself.

An elderly lady in line turned to her husband and asked, "What do they call this thing?"

"I believe they call it a computer," he replied cautiously.

"Com-pew-ter," she said, pronouncing the word slowly. "I'll have to remember that."

At the time, giant main frame computers were housed in air-conditioned rooms and tended by technicians in white lab coats. In 1943, IBM chair Thomas Watson predicted "a world market for maybe five computers." A 1949 *Mechanics Illustrated* article predicted that the size of a computer would likely be kept to 1.5 tons. By the late 1970s, Ken Olson, president of Digital Equipment assured us there was "no reason for individuals to have computers in their homes."

By the 1980s, all that had changed. The personal computer was taking its place on desktops in offices and homes around the world. Not to be left behind—technologically, at least—I signed up for my first computer class, one offered in the evening at the local university. It took half the class period for the students to get on the same page, so to speak. Just getting our floppy disks programmed and the computers booted was a major task. We learned the hard way to "save early and save often."

Our professor assured us that should we want to purchase a personal computer, we would never need more than twenty megabytes of hard drive space. That seemed a bit excessive, but being a professor, we figured he was also a visionary. Today we measure our home computing capacity in gigabytes, or more, and look to new digital possibilities never dreamed of, either by my professor or the skeptic at the Fair.

It is a quantum leap from spitting out birth date information to fixing microchips of information inside humans. I read that a microchip implanted behind the ear might someday improve our memories. What a relief for those of us who go through mental gymnastics just to keep up with our eyeglasses! With such technology, we could at last call up long-forgotten Shakespearean quotes or the location of the car keys.

Better yet, the hidden chip could prompt public speakers, making it unnecessary to rely on notes. You could throw away your business cards because your personal microchip would scan faces and record names. How wonderful! Never again would you have to say, "I know your face, but I can't put a name with it."

We can see change as a challenge to the status quo, a threat to our beliefs, relationships, and routines. Or we can embrace innovation and explore its opportunities.

Sudden and Devastating Change

Not all change is technological; some is all too personal. Life-jarring events start with phrases like: There has been an accident . . . Your test shows a lump . . . I'm moving out . . . Your wife is fine, but the baby has . . . Mom, we need to talk . . . I know you've been with us for twenty years, but . . .

Psychologists tell us that when we experience any one of the following traumas within a given year, we have the potential for deep emotional stress and upheaval.

1. The death, divorce, or separation of a spouse
2. The loss of a child or close relative
3. The loss of a job or the change of a job
4. A move to another city
5. The loss of a home because of finances or destruction
6. A disabling injury or illness
7. Major surgery
8. A radical change in your financial situation
9. Loss of a close friend
10. Retirement

Now, as I read the list, I think of those months following the plane crash when my life seemed shattered beyond repair by some of those very events. I was immediately thrust into a position of deciding if I would take the seat in the U. S. Senate should my husband be elected posthumously.

As I pondered my decision, I felt like the swim mom, who year after year had cheered on her kids at their practice sessions and swim contests. One day she found herself standing on the end of the diving board, having to decide if she would take her own advice and make the plunge. It's lonely at the end of the diving board. The chances of doing a belly flop instead of a swan dive are too great. Like the swim mom, my alternative to diving was to turn back and walk down the ladder, unwilling to test myself or the things I believed to be true. Had I refused, I would have regretted it all my life.

Going to Washington moved me from one shaky and uncertain world into another. The two-year period that framed the 107th Congress in which I served was called "A Time Like No Other." Floor leader Tom Daschle wrote a book by that title, describing the historic session that included a disputed presidential election, the 9/11 terrorist attacks, the decision to go to war in Iraq, and the anthrax mailings.

While serving in the U. S. Senate, I regularly maintained a ten- to twelve-hour work day that included traveling and speaking on weekends. Such a rigorous schedule allowed no time to feel sorry for myself. My personal sorrow was overshadowed by our nation's peril. "I look back and wonder how I got over," the old spiritual declares. I have those feelings as I write these words.

I know now that we must be willing to bear our grief like an ancient traveler assigned to carry a heavy burden for reasons he knows not. He is unaware that there is a tiny hole in the sack and the sand within is slowly trickling out with each step of his journey. At first, it is all he can do to heave the cumbersome load. But as he shoulders the burden each day, the weight lessens.

Eventually, he can stand straight and walk more easily, his eyes no longer cast downward. In time, he gains the assurance and strength of one who has traveled the road and is ready to help others struggling with similar burdens.

Grief, sorrow, and despair are common to each of us in some measure. But, like the night, our despondency is not meant to be permanent. Events can shatter our understanding, but gradually a new day comes, replacing the old with light and hope. Each deliberate step, each decision, each forced smile helps turn back the darkness and hastens the dawn.

The Psalmist wrote, "Weeping may endure the night, but joy comes in the morning." This is more than the recognition that time heals. Joy goes further; it overpowers heartache and despair. In time, peace settles over the heart like a warm blanket comforting the soul. We are renewed.

Letting Loose

From time to time, life forces us to let go of something we prize or someone we cherish. We discover that anything we can hold in our hand can be lost; only what we hold in our hearts endures. It is a hard lesson.

As I try to adjust to a body, a family, and a world in transition, I think of the Serenity Prayer offered years ago by theologian Reinhold Niebuhr. Its simple but vital message has become the inspiration for songwriters and self-help groups worldwide. "God, give us grace to accept with serenity the things that cannot be changed, the courage to change the things that should be changed, and the wisdom to distinguish the one from the other."

Change is natural and necessary, but it need not be unnerving. "If nothing ever changed, there'd be no butterflies."

You Can't Go Home Again

There are things you just can't do in life.
You can't beat the phone company,
you can't make a waiter see you until he's ready to see you,
and you can't go home again.

—Bill Bryson, author

Every holiday season my thoughts drift back to family gatherings and my mother's wonderful home-cooked meals. My favorite was her spoon bread—a treat she reserved for Thanksgiving and Christmas. The wonderful egg and cornmeal concoction was a Southern delicacy from her childhood days in Virginia. It was always the last dish out of the oven and a signal that we should gather quickly at the dinner table.

After her death, I found the recipe among her many cookbooks and kitchen notes. The handwritten card was yellowed with age and stains of batter dropped during the preparation of those meals of yesteryear. I have tried to replicate the dish, but no matter how hard I try, my spoon bread never matches my memories. Ditto for the potato salad, vegetable soup, and turkey dressing. I suppose Thomas Wolfe was right. In his novel *You Can't Go Home Again*, he reminds us that we can't go back home to family, to friends, or to old sights, sounds, and tastes that were once familiar to us.

Still, that doesn't stop me from trying to recapture snippets of bygone times. I still have a fondness for Tuesdays, because it was my mother's day off. When I was in grade school, she and I went shopping along F Street in Washington. I called it "Uptown Tuesday." It was a forty-five-minute bus and streetcar ride to get there, but the time passed quickly as we chatted all the way.

After a few hours of shopping, we'd lunch at the S&W Cafeteria, where they dished up such 1940s favorites as tuna noodle bake, chicken pot pie, chipped beef on toast, succotash, pineapple upside down cake, and Boston cream pie. Then, it was on to the Capitol Theater for the matinee. In addition to the movie, we were entertained by live organ music, group singing, and a vaudeville show.

For me, Uptown Tuesday was a special treat because Mama and I were doing the things we both loved: talking, laughing, walking, singing, shopping, and eating. The last time I was on F Street, it was to take my family to the Spy Museum, which cost $18 a ticket. It simply didn't compare to what we got for 75 cents at the old Capitol Theater.

A Whiff of the Past

Though I now live in St. Louis, I still experience a flash of nostalgia when I go to Soulard Market, the vibrant outdoor market that brims with sounds and aromas. The colorful stalls remind me of Washington's Eastern Market, where my parents used to buy a fluttering chicken in the 1930s and '40s from the stack of wooden coops.

St. Louis' Soulard Market not only has live poultry, it also has live music; Amish-made breads, cakes, and cheeses; exotic plants and herbs; a variety of sausages; and vegetables from artichokes to zucchinis. Fish, fowl, fruits, flowers, and free kittens—they are all there in the open market.

One day as my daughter, her husband, and I navigated the stalls, I was distracted by a vendor offering a wide array of greens. I'm not talking lettuce; I mean the kind of greens you cook. He had turnip greens, collards, kale, mustard greens, and some I didn't recognize.

As a child, I was introduced to Southern-style greens by my grandparents. They ate them at least twice a week—perhaps because the leafy vegetable was cheap. The dish was also simple to prepare, and Granny was not an adventuresome cook. She would first wash the leaves, removing any large veins, and then stuff them into a large pot. Adding a little water, a meaty ham hock, and seasonings, she'd plop the lid on and go back to listening to the radio soap operas.

A couple of hours later the wilted greens were ready to eat. She served them with cornbread to mop up the *pot-likker*, the nutritious juice that comes from the slow cooking. Granny didn't know it, but those mixed greens were chock-full of vitamins A and C and were low in calories. Today we realize that dark green, leafy vegetables, along with blueberries and red wine, top the list of antioxidant-loaded foods.

Despite all the benefits, few in my family will cook or eat greens. I admit that it requires a special tolerance for the smell that not everyone has developed. That's why I have been reluctant to prepare them in my St. Louis condo, thinking there might be a city ordinance against air pollution that would apply.

Even so, I stood in line to purchase several varieties to cook with a ham hock I had in the freezer. There's a special terminology surrounding any discussion of greens, so I said to the vendor, "I want a mess o' greens."

He smiled, no doubt sensing that I knew my greens.

"How many you feedin'?" he asked.

"Just me," I said, "but I want some leftovers."

"A grocery sack feeds four," he said with authority.

I knew from watching Granny that a "mess o' greens" cooks down to about a fourth, or less, of what you put in the pot.

"Okay, then, I'll take a half-sack," I said.

The young lady behind me, wearing a tastefully coordinated linen outfit with Birkenstock sandals, was eyeing the arugula and shiitake mushrooms.

"Is that stuff really good to eat?" she asked with a slight wrinkle of her nose.

The two African American women behind her laughed.

"Lord, you don't know good until you eat greens," one said.

The arugula woman may have been curious, but she was not about to take a culinary risk based on our advice.

When I showed my daughter the half-bag of leaves, she asked, "What are you going to cook those in?"

"Well," I replied, "you know what Louis Armstrong said when asked how he cooked red beans and rice: 'First, get a pot half the size of a tuba . . . ' "

"But now that you live in a condo, you don't have a pot half the size of a tuba. You gave it to me," she said.

"Oh, that's right," I replied innocently. "Will you take these greens home and cook them for me?"

"Nothing doing," she replied. "We're cooking fish and veggies on the grill tonight. Why don't you come eat with us?"

"Okay," I said. "I'll bring the greens."

"We're going to have plenty to eat," she replied with a patronizing air. "Why don't you just keep those for yourself, since you enjoy them so much more than the rest of us."

And that's what I did. I ate them with great delight, like one would secretly devour a box of Godiva chocolate—but without the guilt and with lots of memories of my grandmother's kitchen.

Things I've Always Wanted

I keep a mental list of "Things I've Always Wanted, But Never Got." We've all made such a list, but most of us outgrew our longing for items we once thought so desirable. I'm embarrassed to say it, but I still have a few unusual "wants" that I have clung to over the years. They are ridiculous, but here goes . . .

I have always wanted an ice shaver. No, it's not a device for freezing off unwanted body hair. Once upon a time, it was the way "summer snowballs" were made.

One of my earliest memories was going into a mom-and-pop grocery in northeast Washington to buy a syrupy, flavored snowball made from freshly shaven ice. Almost as delightful as eating this frosty concoction was watching it being prepared. It began when Mr. Carney, the store owner, grabbed a pair of ice tongs from off the wall and used it to lift a large block of ice into a sink.

Holding my mother's hand, I would watch wide-eyed as he ran the blade side of a small, cast iron box across the frozen block. When the container filled with ice shavings, he would pop a mound of the mushy ice into a paper cone and douse it with your preference of green, red, purple, or orange syrup. All for only three cents. Mama let me count out the three pennies into Mr. Carney's huge, fleshy hand. My first commercial transaction.

I envied Mr. Carney's ice shaver. I was four years old and wanted so much to have one of my very own, so I could make snowballs any time and for anybody. (How I would handle the twenty-pound block of ice,

I didn't figure. At the time, the nifty ice shaver seemed to be the only necessary requirement.)

I would never own, or even handle, an ice shaver. After we moved from the neighborhood, I never saw one again—that is, until I wandered through an antique store many years later.

There it sat on the counter, waiting to be discovered. I knew it had to be Mr. Carney's ice shaver. It looked just like I remembered.

I summoned my grandson, who was waiting impatiently at the door.

"Do you know what this is?" I said excitedly.

"It looks like a metal match box," he ventured.

"No," I said, "this is an ice shaver."

"Okay. Can we go now?"

"No. I have *got* to have this. I've always wanted one," I said, arguing my case for buying such a useless device.

"If I can find where to buy a block of ice and some colored syrup, we could make snowballs anytime we want them," I said.

He laughed.

I was hurt by his scorn.

"Believe me, this is better than Baskin-Robbins or Ben & Jerry's," I protested.

"Grandma! You are talking about ice and syrup—that's just a Popsicle."

I paid him no heed.

Turning to the clerk, I said, "How much is this item?"

He rubbed his chin for awhile and rolled the piece around in his fingers before answering.

"You know, they don't make these anymore," he said slowly. "Most people don't know what this is or how to use it."

"I know," I said all too eagerly.

"It's the only one I've ever had in the store. I'll need at least $20 for it," he declared, turning to deal briefly with another customer.

"Grandma, I can't believe you'd pay $20 bucks for that . . . that whatever-it-is," my grandson whispered.

"*Ice shaver*," I said. "It's an authentic, honest-to-goodness ice shaver like they used to make snowballs with when I was a little girl."

"Okay, but did you know that SpongeBob SquarePants makes a snow cone kit that does the same thing for only $14.99?"

I ignored his inappropriate comparison.

"I'll see you in the car, young man. I'm doing some serious negotiating here." Turning back, the clerk inquired, "Well, can I wrap that up for you?"

I Agonized

I sighed and fondled the little metal box in my hand. I made a few long, slow movements across an imaginary ice block. I opened the trap door that dislodged the scrapings just as I remembered Mr. Carney doing. I could almost taste the cool, grapey flavor of the purple topping—my favorite.

After a few wistful moments, I gently placed the little box back onto the counter and said sadly, "I'll think about it."

"You shouldn't wait too long. Lots of people want these old ice shavers," he replied.

"I don't doubt it," I said agreeably, but in my heart I knew that no one was looking for Mr. Carney's ice shaver but me. And, for a brief moment, I had found it. Now that the shaver was mine to have, I could find absolutely no reason to justify the purchase.

I told myself that serious ice crushing is done with a refrigerator attachment, not with Mr. Carney's scraper or even a SpongeBob SquarePants kit. In the end, reason won the day, but remembrance brightened it. How wonderful when sensations of childhood can be prompted by such simple objects from the past. These marvelous moments are infrequent, but they are priceless and definitely non-shareable.

Having learned from that experience, I no longer search for another object that I once yearned for: my very own light table—one of those wood-framed boxes with glass on top and a light bulb underneath. With the development of Photoshop, I have outgrown my need to cut and paste pages in preparation for printing.

Still, that didn't stop me from ogling the six-foot-square professional light table I saw being used in a stained glass shop recently. I started to make the owner an offer, until I realized I would have to remove my car from the garage to find six feet of open space.

Recently, my kids took pity on me and indulged my longing for another of the "Things I've Always Wanted." I now have a farm *windmill!* Yes, one Christmas I got a truckload of assorted metal parts that came from an old dismantled windmill—with only some pieces missing. It took nearly a year to have it re-assembled and installed, but I now have a rotating windmill to watch from my kitchen window.

Some things are worth the wait.

Finding My Way Home

Some years ago, I returned to the neighborhood in which I lived as a child. Had I heeded the words of Heraclitus, I would have known that "No man ever steps in the same river twice for it is not the same river and he is not the same man."

Ignoring the warnings of the ancient Greeks, I loaded my reluctant teenagers into the car so I'd have someone to bore with my childhood memories and to challenge my recollections. It had been years since I'd seen the old neighborhood where my parents and I had lived for fifteen years.

As we drove slowly along S Street with its row of neatly-kept brick homes, I spotted a For Sale sign in one yard. It reminded me that these semi-detached houses built following the Depression were originally offered to first-time home buyers, such as my family, for less than $6,000. Today they are selling for a quarter of a million dollars.

"Are you sure you'll know which one it is?" asked a smart aleck in the backseat, after noting the similarity of the houses. My family had heard me say that as a youngster, living in a neighborhood of alphabetized streets, I had to learn my ABCs just to find my way home. I assured them that I could find my way in the dark even now.

As we approached my old house, my eyes went immediately to the window where my grandmother would have been sitting, awaiting my return from school each day. Now the curtains were tightly pulled.

As I looked about, I was saddened by all that was missing:

Gone was the rose trellis that my father built and, with it, the array of American Beauty roses, the envy of every neighbor on the block.

It was Monday. Yet in the backyard there were no billowing bed sheets pinned onto sagging clothes lines supported by bamboo poles.

Gone, too, was the squeaky metal glider with the cushions that stuck to your legs on a sweltery summer day.

"What do you expect to see?" one of my kids commented nonchalantly.

I didn't say, but in my mind, I wanted to go home again, if just for a moment in time. I wanted to see Daddy in front of the house tinkering with the engine of our Oldsmobile. My mother in the kitchen baking a chocolate cake. My grandmother humming a tune in her rocking chair. My cousins playing ball in the alley.

Because it was summer, I expected the wool rugs would be stored and the woven, summer carpet in place. My bowl of guppies would be pressing against the fishbowl wanting to be fed. The elderly next-door neighbor would be sitting on the front porch crocheting a colorful, lace border around a handkerchief. The bowl of wax fruit sitting atop Mama's hand-made tablecloth would be undergoing a slow meltdown in the summer heat.

It was not like that at all. And never would be again.

I toyed with the idea of going up to the front door and knocking. I would introduce myself as the original resident and then reveal all the wonderful memories associated with the little brick home.

"What if you get a blank stare, a laugh, or a slammed door?" one of my tormentors in the backseat asked.

He was right. Still, I wondered how the house was furnished, especially what the living room looked like now. I remember the 1940s when Mama bought The Sofa, as it would be forever known—though my grandmother called it The Long Chair. We didn't make many big-ticket purchases, so when she bought The Sofa and two side chairs, it was a historic family moment.

Some families have religious shrines in their homes; we had The Sofa. Company was allowed to sit on it; family only looked at it adoringly. Sometimes I would sneak a sit, only to hear my mother call out from the kitchen, *"Get off The Sofa!"* One season she covered it in a stiff plastic, which allowed us to sit down but was so unpleasant I didn't want to any longer.

Mama proudly described the style as "Eighteenth Century," not that she knew what that meant. It had a camel back, rolled arms, and carved, turned legs. (I later learned these are called cabriole legs.) It was terribly out of place in a fourteen-foot square living room in a row house, but Mama and her friends adored it.

Without knowing it I bonded with this relic, even taking it into my farm home after my mother's death. It is still in great condition, but it resides in storage today. I don't know what to do with it. I have thought of a burning ceremony, like when disposing of an old flag. I have decided to leave the decision to my grandchildren, who have no attachment to The Sofa and can deal with it more rationally.

I now know you can't pull up the past like a stored document on a computer. Nor can our recollections be downloaded to others. We have only "the mystic chords of memory" to give us a hint of former times, and those are often muted.

We can *look* back, but we cannot *go* back. All we can say is, "I once was there. I learned, I loved, I grew, I moved on."

In my case, I like to think that I did more than just grow. With the tender care of loving parents, I blossomed. I can look back and smile, knowing that I was blessed by a nurturing home, church, and community.

I hoped that my own kids would someday find their own stroll down memory lane as meaningful. But for the moment, they were bored by my reverie.

One piped up, "It's getting late; I'm hungry."

The others chimed in.

"Me, too," I said, snapping out of my trance.

"There's this great deli nearby. Just keep going for a few blocks and take a left."

We found the place. It had become a supermarket.

Every Contact Leaves a Trace

Spread love everywhere you go: first of all in your own house.
Give love to your children, to your wife or husband,
to a next-door neighbor . . . ·
Let no one ever come to you without leaving better and happier.
— *Mother Teresa*

Ahhh . . . the 1950s—a time when American families gathered around their black-and-white television screens, awaiting the next episode of *Leave It to Beaver*, the ongoing saga of the Cleaver family.

In this portrayal of the perfect family, Ward Cleaver was the father who came home every night after a hard day at the office and dealt creatively and patiently with any problems on the domestic front. June, the model housewife, was always there for her family, dishing up a favorite dinner casserole or some wholesome advice for her sons, Wally and Beaver.

Life at 211 Pine Street in Mayfield, Ohio, was a myth, impossible to duplicate. Problems were solved in a thirty-minute time frame, each show ending on a happy note. It was a fantasy world, but we loved it, and we benefited from the parenting lessons incorporated in the series. Like an ancient morality play, the show gave us insight into dealing with our own family troubles.

Traditionally, a family takes on the shape needed to nurture the young, aged, and infirmed among its members. As I looked at some photos recently, it occurred to me that my family has evolved dramatically. I started out as an only child, with two parents, one set of grandparents, and an assortment of cousins. Being family, we made room for each other in times of need. When I was born during the Depression, my parents and I, an uncle, aunt, cousin, and two grandparents all lived under the same roof and shared expenses. Over the years, we took in relatives—nieces, nephews, and cousins—who were getting started in the workplace or had fallen on hard times.

After I married and had children, my mother died, and my father moved in with my family. He lived with us for the last seven years of his life. I grew up believing that the worst thing that could happen to someone was to be left alone in distress, hardship, sickness, or old age.

The decision to share a home—including bathroom and closet space—with another person requires some adjustments. Whether it's moving in with family or helping a friend needing temporary housing, we are forced to change our ways. My father was in his late seventies when he joined our six-member household. At the time, none of us had any idea how the new arrangement would work out day to day.

We furnished my father's new bedroom with the things from his former home. We shuffled items in the refrigerator to make room for his diabetic foods. We even began eating healthier meals at predictable times because of his requirements. He surprised me by doing little things that lightened my day. Often when I came home from the office, the kitchen floor was swept, the table set, the dog fed, the plants watered, and the laundry folded.

Looking back on those seven years, I realize it took effort from all of us to make the arrangement work. Sociologist Margaret Mead considered it important that we have three-generational families. Now I know why. The daily interaction required patience, trust, and respect. The experience connected us in ways that build strong families, forming a bond that we would have achieved in no other way.

The Many Faces of Family

Families take on different forms as people coalesce around those they love and need. John and Mary, for instance, may each have a child by a previous marriage and one of their own. Elizabeth and Jill may live together with an adoptive son. Henry and Mabel may have taken in their two grandchildren, while Charles and Sarah have several foster children. I marvel at the family with eighteen children featured on a television documentary, but I also admire those who adopt special needs youngsters. All are families attempting to nurture those within their households.

Drawing others into our family circle can be a learning opportunity as well as a great joy. I discovered that many years ago when our family unofficially "adopted" a mainland Chinese professor studying in this country and away from his own family for two years. He had a fascinating background, having endured the hardships of the Cultural Revolution. During that bitter and divisive time, he was taken from his university classroom and forced to dig ditches in the countryside. He had survived the ordeal with no hint of bitterness. As we shared meals, trips, and family celebrations, Mr. Cheng became a part of our extended family. He was missing his own family, so we loaned him ours.

My family accompanied him to the airport for his return to China. As we drove home, I felt like we had lost a member of our family. I recall my teenage son, drying his eyes sadly and saying, "I loved that man." We all did, because he had grown to be a part of our lives.

Child Rearing Ain't for Sissies

If there is a surefire method for raising children, it is not widely known or even agreed upon. Experts have unlocked many of the mysteries of the universe, but not this one. Like the cure for the common cold, the secret of transforming a pint-sized tyrant into an operational adult has eluded our best efforts. There is even disagreement as to how we measure a successful outcome.

Unlike our toaster ovens, children come without an instruction manual or guarantee. We are left to follow our parental instincts. Even so, there are things we can do to improve our odds of success. Children are by nature imitators, looking to adults for signals about what is right or wrong. Being copycats, they mimic what they see and hear from those around them, often doing so unconsciously.

Years after my mother's death, I hear myself saying the same phrases with the same inflections that she used. I tilt my head just as she did; I laugh the same way. I didn't do so as a child, but I do now. Growing up, I had no desire to imitate my parents, who I often saw as old-fashioned in their thinking and habits. Apparently, I picked up many of their attitudes and mannerisms—at least that's what my kids tell me.

If parents are being copied, either consciously or unconsciously, it might be well to consider our ways more carefully. At best, we are all imperfect models. I make these observations knowing that any theory about childrearing can be proven wrong. I look at my father, one of eleven children, most of whom were grown by the time he came along. His mother died shortly after the birth of her last child, leaving his father with three young sons at home. Later, when their farm house burned, there were no resources with which to rebuild.

A nearby family adopted the infant, and my father (age eight at the time) and his older brother were taken in by a local widow, who needed help with her farm chores. Surprisingly, my dad turned out to be a good-humored, honest, and caring person, unafraid of hard work. "You can't let life get'cha down," he'd say. It was a philosophy he had certainly learned the hard way.

Sadly, we all know stories of disadvantaged children who didn't fare so well. We also know situations where kids were given every opportunity and yet failed to measure up.

So what's a parent to do?

Recognizing our status as role models is a good beginning. Because children tend to copy our conduct, habits, speech, and opinions, it is important to be consistent. Whenever we step out of our "role," children are quick to notice the deviation. The "don't do as I do, do as I say" conundrum is not a long-range child-rearing policy. Effective parenting requires a "show and tell" approach. What we *show* and what we *tell* should match.

This doesn't ensure complete success, but it certainly ups the odds. Having done our best, there is no need to browbeat ourselves. Even the Almighty has difficulty with His creations not measuring up to their potential. Why, then, should we expect to outdo His success? Still, He doesn't give up trying; nor should we.

The Eight Muscle-builders for Families

Regardless of a family's makeup or number, there are eight muscle-builders for strengthening families. All strong families "exercise" these qualities:

1. *Love.* Mother Teresa's advice to "do small things with great love" is especially true for families. She wrote, "Spread love everywhere you go: first of all in your own house. Give love to your children, to your wife or husband, to a next door neighbor . . . Let no one ever come to you without leaving better and happier. Be the living expression of God's kindness—kindness in your face, kindness in your eyes, kindness in your smile, kindness in your warm greeting." Love is the glue—the bond—that cements a true family. But love is not all huggy-kissy. Sometimes families must be willing to

exhibit a tough love for those who continue to harm themselves and others.

2. *Respect.* We say some of the meanest, most insulting things to those who live under our own roofs. Name-calling, fault-finding, dredging up past failings, and verbal or physical abuse violate our feelings as human beings. The requirement that one should fight fair is especially true of families expressing disagreement with one another. I have a number of friends who describe themselves as growing up in a "dysfunctional family." Most of them recognized the situation early in life and worked mightily to make sure they did not repeat the pattern. But, all too often, abusive behavior stemming from alcohol, jealousy, anger, neglect, and favoritism leaves permanent wounds.

3. *Acceptance.* We may share the same DNA, but we are not all alike. Allowing for those differences requires a high level of tolerance and patience. A friend with a difficult family member told me that she has developed a way of handling her father's insensitive remarks. "I laugh it off whenever possible," she said. She will not allow the parent to "get to her," to make her angry or bitter. She admits that her attitude has not yet changed her father but, she says confidently, "At least, I'm not becoming like him."

4. *Security.* The home should provide a safe haven to which family members can return. Within its walls each should feel protected from the pressures and hostility of the world. Families with a member who is subject to

severe temper outbursts, abusive acts, or threatening language need immediate professional help. When a loved one is physically ill, you seek treatment and work toward a recovery. The same must happen when someone is repeatedly injured, mentally or physically, in your home. No one should have to feel that a loved one is a threat to the well-being of the family.

5. *Communication.* Even in the best of families, there are times when we under-perform. We pick on each other. We magnify small faults or give too little praise. We hold grudges, complain too freely, or treat each other unfairly. We are quick to point out when we are over-worked, underappreciated, or ignored. Fortunately, most families have developed non-hostile ways of handling their problems. One way to do that is to follow the Psalmist's advice: "Do not let the sun go down upon your wrath." Even the ancients had figured out that it is not good to let a matter fester overnight.

6. *Encouragement.* Maya Angelou wrote, "External events, colleagues, associates, friends, and hostile forces will bring enough to cry about. So as often as possible laugh and hug somebody." Successful families have a supportive, can-do attitude that helps members build on their strengths, calm their fears, and overcome their weakness. Every family has some common sayings that reflect its attitudes. I wish I had a nickel for every time I heard my father say: "It's no use crying over spilt milk." It was a recognition that bad and unpreventable things happen in life, but you don't get discouraged or

give up. No matter what happens, you pick yourself up and keep going. It was a valuable lesson taught repeatedly by the little incidents that occurred in daily life.

7. *Trust.* Knowing that we are there for each other in good times and bad is the essence of a thriving family. When we trust each other, we achieve a closeness that helps us resolve problems and disputes. Families that share common values are also more resilient, making them better able to handle a crisis.

8. *Don't forget the fun!* Being able to laugh and enjoy each other's company goes a long way to improving the emotional well-being of family members. Writer Anne Lamott calls laughter "carbonated holiness" that wells up and spills over, refreshing every occasion. Strong families look for ways to have fun and to share common values. Daily meals together, story times for youngsters, hobbies, holidays, vacations, celebrations, and religious and community activities help to forge lasting and loving relationships.

According to the French criminologist, Edmund Locard, "Every contact leaves a trace." That is true in forensic science, but it's also true of our contacts with each other. Our lives must touch. Only then are we safe and fulfilled.

Our Family's Marriage Blessing

I offered this wedding prayer first at the outdoor wedding of my son Tom and his bride, Lisa. When my daughter Robin and Juan Carlos married, I repeated it again—but with a preface. The previous year Robin had been through chemotherapy for breast cancer. All that was behind her; she was now a lovely, joyful bride.

"To Robin and Juan Carlos:

"I can't tell you how many times I have watched the film *Princess Bride*. I cry as Buttercup and Westley overcome the most horrendous circumstances with nothing more than true love.

"We are amused by the corny sentiments the film portrays, but secretly each of us hopes that such love really exists. St. Paul tells us that it does. And that those who find it are the most blessed of human beings. He describes true love as kind, patient, and enduring—the gift of a benevolent God.

"The year preceding a marriage would normally be the happiest and most carefree for a couple in love. For Robin and Juan Carlos, it turned into a stern test—one that would have destroyed some relationships. But Robin and Juan Carlos not only endured, they prevailed. And today marks their victory.

"Let us pray:

"Our Father, we gather before this altar of ancient rocks, surrounded by soft breezes, flowered walks, the gentle sounds of nature and precious memories.

"As the sun drifts behind the horizon, giving promise of a new day, we need not invoke Your presence, for You are surely here.

"Our hearts rejoice with Robin and Juan Carlos as they affirm their love for one another.

"In the solitude and beauty of this place, two lives have become one. We ask you to consecrate this union and the love that brings them together.

"As their new lives unfold, we ask that you dwell with them.

"Give each of them strength of spirit, so they may honor the vows they made this day.

"Help them to respect one another's likes and dislikes, opinions and beliefs, hopes, dreams, and fears, even though they may not always understand them.

"Grant them humility, kindness, patience, forgiveness, and trust, not only for each other, but for all whose lives they touch.

"May the love You have implanted in their hearts inspire kind words, tenderness of feelings, and concern each for the other.

"Help them to realize that there is a design and purpose in life and that no matter what they may face, their oneness makes them far stronger than either of them alone.

"With our families here assembled, we thank You for our children, who have blessed our lives, and for their love that overflows, filling each of our hearts as well.

"We pledge to encourage and strengthen the new beginning that marks this day.

"Hear us now, O Lord, as we pray Your blessing upon these, our children. May Your goodness smile upon them and abide with them in all their ways.

"May the joy and peace, which only God can give and which cannot be taken away by any happening in this world, be yours today and in all of life's tomorrows.

"Amen."

Words Paint Pictures
in Your Head

*Our great men have written words of wisdom to be used when
hardship must be faced: life obliges us with hardship, so the
words of wisdom shouldn't go to waste.*
 —*Sheldon Harnick, lyricist,* Fiddler on the Roof

My fascination with words did not come from having grown up in a literary setting. Actually, the only books in my home were a Bible and a set of blue 1930s-era encyclopedias, with one volume missing.

As a teenager, I was thrilled to receive a hardback Webster's dictionary as a birthday gift. Discovering a word or phrase that captured my imagination, I would write it in a notebook, along with its meaning. I found that some words inspired me, while others made me sad, and still others painted pictures or exuded strength. That was especially true of the Bible; it contained the most heavenly sounding language I had ever read.

I was also mesmerized by crossword puzzles, a pursuit that my grandfather encouraged. A carpenter by trade, Granddaddy came home each evening with a copy of the *Washington Daily News* tucked under his arm. After dinner, he would retire to his easy chair, the one with the worn arms and doily-covered headrest. After reading the news, he would use his pen knife to sharpen a pencil to a fine point, and he would then spend the rest of the evening working the puzzle. I often joined him and learned the thrill of completing a word task, using terms that I used only in crossword puzzles. I cherished those times with my grandfather. It was as though we shared a secret language that only the two of us understood. (To this day, when I have a few idle moments, I browse *The Word Detective* on the Internet just for fun.)

Professor Henry Higgins would have been distraught over the many quaint expressions used in my home when I was a kid. My father never gave up using the term *ice box* for refrigerator, *parasol* for umbrella, and *chimley* for chimney. He knew the proper usage but defiantly held to the expressions he had heard as a youngster. (It was only after he died that I discovered chimley was once a perfectly acceptable English word. Sir Walter Scott in his book *Rob Roy* refers to a "kirk with a chimley in it." I regret that I was never able to share that with him; he would have felt so vindicated.)

My parents substituted *carry* for *drive*. My father's response to the question, "Where have you been?" might be, "I carried your mother to the grocery store." He didn't drive her; she was carried. When someone asked how he was doing, often his reply was "Fair to middlin.'"

As a youngster, I noticed that my relatives still living in rural Virginia observed a quaint differentiation between objects close at hand and those farther away. The word *there* was used if a thing was within a few feet or so, as in, "Hand me that book over there." In referring to something more distant or out of sight, they would say, "See that barn over yonder?"

I never figured out what the distance was that triggered the usage of *over yonder*—though Shakespeare used *yonder* in pointing to objects in the same room: "What light through yonder window breaks?" *Down yonder* seemed to denote something below eye level or southward, as in the song *Way Down Yonder in New Orleans.*

My grandmother would often say, "I'll do that *prez-nee.*" I was grown before I figured out that the word was a distortion of *presently* and a proper English usage. She would call someone with little ambition *trifling* or a *ne'er-do-well*, especially if he or she lacked *gumption*—a needed quality for any successful undertaking. If you pretended to be *bad off*, you might be accused of *poor mouthin'*.

When I asked too many questions, my grandmother might ask, "Why are you being so vexing?" Or if I was *plundering* through a dresser drawer, I was urged not to be so *meddlesome*. If I moved too slowly or wasted time, I was *piddlin' around*.

My grandfather used two words from the King James era: *deef* (deaf) and *bile* (boil). He often simplified verbs, for instance, using *et* (eat) for all the tenses.

Lord willin' was a phrase that bracketed any statement of future intent, as in "I'll be there next Tuesday, Lord willin'." Anything short of that was to presume upon the will of the Almighty.

Affixing the name of God to any form of profanity was *taking the Lord's name in vain* and a violation of the Calvinistic teachings passed down from my Protestant forbearers. Frustration could be expressed by prefacing a sentence with *I do declare*, as in, "I do declare, I don't know what's come over that boy."

But a statement of surprise or pleasure might be rendered *Lord-a-mercy*, as in "Lord-a-mercy, what a rain we had last night," or "Lord knows, I'm telling the gospel truth."

One could *swear to heaven*, over some trivial matter, but not *swear to God*. We were of the Baptist faith, which was pronounced *Bab-tiss* and is still pronounced that way by most people in the South.

A woman might be *ugly as a mud fence, madder than an old wet hen, fat as a pig, dressed up like Hester's pet pig* or *all gussied up*. Derelicts were described as *crooked as a dog's hind leg* or *drunk as a skunk*, while the stingy were *tight as Dick's hat band*. (Never figured out who Dick was to be immortalized in such a way). An angry person was *fit to be tied*.

A matter of no consequence was *not worth a hill of beans* and a no-good individual *not worth shooting*. A man's deep, dark eyes might look like *two burnt holes in a blanket*. An inquiry might be prefaced with "What in the Sam Hill are you doing?"

If you got too *uppity*, you were *putting on airs*. Anyone who had made himself *scarce*, might be greeted with "I ain't seen you in a coon's age."

An angry person might be described as *hotter than a two dollar pistol* while someone comfortable was *snug as a bug in a rug*. An item in short supply was, *scarcer than hen's teeth*. Someone who had overeaten was *full as a tick*; an underfed person was *skinny as a rail*. It might be said of a person in ill health, "She looks poorly."

Someone could be *slow as molasses in January* or *fast as greased lightning*. A person could be *grinning like a Chessy cat* (a variation of Cheshire cat), as *crazy as a June bug*, or *honest as the day is long*. If you had a stomachache, you might be *bound up*.

Bless your heart, was a versatile expression that covered just about any situation. Most often, it was used as a verbal pat on the head. You could say anything you wanted to about a person if you used the phrase to soften the blow, as in, "He doesn't have the brains God gave a goose, bless his heart."

Y'all was commonplace and so handy that I still use it today, though I often hear my kids say *you guys*. Proper usage demands that *y'all* be used in the plural rather than when referring to an individual.

Reckon was often used for *suppose*, as in "You reckon he'll be here for dinner?" or "I don't reckon so." *Let on* could mean *pretend* or *act*: "She let on she didn't care," or "Don't let on you saw him." An inquiry as to location might be: "Where 'bouts is it?"

Certain inquiries typically brought a predictable response. When someone complimented my father by saying, "Mr. Carpenter, you're looking good," he would invariably respond, "Looks are deceiving." When my grandmother was asked how old she was, she'd always declare, "I'm as old as my gums and a little bit older than my teeth." My cousins and I thought it such an amusing answer that we would ask her age just to hear the response.

If a request seemed to overreach or to be an imposition, it might be met with, "Who was your servant at this time last year?" A smart-aleck reply was, "You were, but you didn't serve your time."

I have carefully purged all these colorful bits of language from my current speech, though occasionally, like Eliza Doolittle, something jumps out from my past to give me away. I still throw the letter *r* into the word "wash," as in "I grew up in *War-shington*."

After years of effort, I now pronounce the words *house, mouse,* and *again* like a proper Midwesterner. Still, I often drop the *g* from a word ending in -*ing* to help move the sentence along faster, or I revert to using the collective pronoun, as in "Why don't *y'all* come over for dinner tonight"—though my parents would have said *supper*.

Romancing the Stone

While traveling in Ireland some years ago, I felt compelled to make the trip to County Cork, the location of Blarney Castle. Each year nearly half a million tourists pay ten euros to kiss an ancient rock embedded in the wall of the six-hundred-year-old castle.

What makes the rock special? Some say it was the rock on which Jacob slept, or the one David hid behind when he was running from King Saul. Others say that the castle owner saved an old woman from drowning. She repaid him by endowing the stone with "magical" powers.

Of course, no one would climb the narrow, twisting stairway, wait in a line, and stand on her head to perform this tricky maneuver without good reason. Supposedly, the rock bestows the gift of eloquent and convincing speech upon all those who "romance the stone."

An Irish ballad from the 19th century makes even greater claims for the rock.

> There is a stone there,
>
> That whoever kisses,
>
> Oh, he never misses
>
> To grow eloquent.
>
> 'Tis he may clamber
>
> To a lady's chamber,
>
> Or become a member
>
> Of Parliament.

For centuries, travelers—from Sir Walter Scott to Winston Churchill to Ronald Reagan—have visited the village of Blarney to pay homage to the old stone in hopes of taking away the gift of eloquence. Reagan obviously thought the stone had bestowed its mystical charm on some American politicians. When the president addressed the Irish Parliament, he referred to the Blarney Stone as the "wellspring of so much American political success."

That appears to be the case in the Carnahan family. I have a picture of my father-in-law, A. S. J. Carnahan, kissing the Blarney Stone when he was a sailor during World War I. Since then, the rest of my family has followed suit. The elder Carnahan went on to become a member of Congress. Before becoming governor, my husband served in the Missouri legislature (as did our son Russ) before being elected to Congress. My daughter Robin, a candidate for the U. S. Senate in 2010, also kissed the stone, so we will see if the rock still holds its elective clout.

When I visited the castle, I had no thought of serving in Congress. I did think the promised gift of eloquence might be useful, even though I had to be hung by the heels over the castle wall to achieve the oratorical blessing. The feat is not like walking up to the Wailing Wall in Jerusalem; the kissing maneuver requires a team effort. You begin by lying on your back, grabbing two iron rails behind you and letting your head drop backward to kiss the rock behind you. An assistant holds your legs and guides you into place.

Finding me awkward to align, my assistant gave me a hearty, downward shove. I felt like my head was going to fall off and roll down the castle wall. I came up out of the hole swinging and muttering less-than-eloquent speech.

While the Blarney Stone legend makes for great tourism, I have discovered that fine speech and fitting words require more than standing on your head and slobbering on a rock.

"Loaded Pistols"

On the playground, we used to say, "Sticks and stones will break my bones, but words will never hurt me." Even then, I knew that was not true. Words can be powerful instruments for good, or they can be what Jean-Paul Sartre called "loaded pistols."

Certain words have the power to change how I feel about myself or a situation. I am inspired by the words *rugged, steadfast, gallant, undaunted, resilient,* and *spunky.* I call them power-wrapped words. For me, they convey strength any time they are used.

Winston Churchill reminded us, "The short words are best and the old words are best of all." I would add that some of the most meaningful statements contain the fewest words. The following list has been called The Most Important Words in the English Language. They are especially well-suited for use in the family and workplace. I have searched for its author to no avail.

The six most important words are: "I was wrong, please forgive me."

The five most important words are: "You did a good job."

The four most important words are: "What is your opinion?"

The three most important words are: "Can I help?"

The two most important words are: "Thank you."

The one most important word is: "You."

The least important word is: "I."

For better or worse, words convey our thoughts. They can lift, or they can level. They can enable, or they can belittle. They can inspire, motivate, and calm, or they can degrade, hurt, and weaken. Use them with caution.

Age Is a Moveable Feast

*The view after seventy is breathtaking. What is lacking is
someone, anyone, of the older generation to whom you can turn
when you want to satisfy your curiosity about some detail of the
landscape of the past. There is no longer any older generation.
You have become it while your mind was mostly on other matters.*
—William Keepers Maxwell Jr.,
from Billie Dyer and Other Stories

I'm lovin' my position atop the totem pole of life. There are few around
to dispute the validity of my recollections. One of the advantages of
growing older is being able to relate an incident in any way we choose,
without fear of being challenged on the details. If some young upstart

dares to dispute your account, he can be put in his place with a quick retort, "Honey, you weren't even born then."

Now, I mean no malice toward the young, or even middle-aged. It's just that they don't have the same reservoir of memory from which to draw. Their wells are far too shallow. Often when I say, "Do you remember when . . . ?" all I get back is a blank stare. I enjoy the company of those whose recollections go back further than the Cuban Missile Crisis—someone who thinks Van Johnson was cute, has an appreciation for *Lili Marlene* played on an accordion, or knows when to use the expression, "hubba, hubba, zing, zing."

For solace I turn to the Internet. Because we now live in the Broadband Age, cyberspace is awash with senior Web wags who regularly e-mail each other on topics of mutual interest. We pass along the most outrageous jokes and stories about the humor we see in aging and the world around us.

I stay connected with my old friends by e-mail, BlackBerry, or instant messaging. But some still need handwritten letters—an ancient ritual that requires stationery, an envelope, a working ballpoint pen, correct postage, a current address, and a trip to the mailbox. Most of these dear hearts are over seventy and don't want to re-train at this point in life. (Fortunately, I still have a few old note cards with flowers on them, though I'm running low.)

Don't get me wrong. I enjoy handwritten letters. For the most part, I toss my IMs and e-mails into the delete bin. But I keep many of the personalized letters—those tender tidings from old friends—because their words are encouraging, complimentary, and worth an occasional re-read.

As you can tell, I have mixed emotions when it comes to connectivity. I am saddened that handwritten notes have become a cultural relic, losing ground to cell phones and laptops. So, I have compromised. Most often I wing my words through cyberspace, but for special occasions, I follow the advice of Wordsworth: "Fill your paper with the breathings of your heart."

My Favorite "Uppers"

When the *Peanuts* character Charlie Brown told Lucy that life has its ups and downs, she replied, "I don't want ups and downs. All I want are ups, ups, ups."

Me, too, Lucy. So, here are a few of my favorite Uppers for Grown-ups.

Keep Up. Stay in touch with life. Be open to new friends and protective of the old ones. Pursue a hobby; hop on the Internet; follow the news; share information; learn something new; listen. Try to make each day different from the previous, even if it's no more than taking the stairs instead of the elevator or shopping in a different grocery. Anything that keeps the mind and body from becoming sluggish is worth the effort. Refuse to give into what writer Pamela Stephenson calls "beigeing down" in clothes, conversation, or interests.

Make Up. Forgiveness is not entirely for the benefit of the forgiven. Yet there are so many good reasons not to forgive. We are hurt—sometimes deeply. Our relative, friend, or coworker is unworthy of our forgiveness. Retaliation seems so necessary. For good reasons, we justify ourselves for not bestowing this most godly of treasures upon another human being.

When Jesus was asked if it was enough to forgive a person seven times, He upped the requirement. He called on us to forgive "seventy times seventy." That is the equivalent of forgiving once a day for thirteen years! In that amount of time, forgiveness would surely be a well-established habit.

Forgiving ourselves for some past failing is often the most difficult. Extended guilt trips are unhealthy. When there is nothing more we can do to make things right, we have to let go of our guilt. Just drop it on God's doorstep; He knows what to do.

Shape Up. The two most important words for "grown-ups" are *keep moving*. Unused muscles atrophy. So use the face muscles regularly for smiles and laughter; the arms for hugs; and the legs for brisk walking.

Work on balance, too. There are simple exercises to do at home that will help keep you from falling. If you literally want to go the second mile, check out your local fitness center or gym. There are people in their eighties working out regularly at the gym where I go several days a week. They are such an inspiration.

Team Up. Connect with family, friends, and neighbors, as well as religious, political, and social organizations. Instead of thinking of yourself as too old, think of yourself as too valuable not to be involved. All of us, regardless of age, like to feel that we are part of something worthwhile.

I visited a number of states as a surrogate speaker for Barack Obama during his presidential campaign. I was surprised at how many seniors were volunteering at their local campaign headquarters. It was delightful to see older people packing in home-baked breads and crockpots of chili. They not only fed the young people and staffers, they also worked alongside them, manning the phones and walking the neighborhoods.

Tune Up. I take my car in regularly for its periodic checkups. It came with a maintenance schedule that I adhere to consistently. Most often it needs only minor tune ups, but sometimes technicians catch a problem before it gets too far along. I must admit I hate to have these checkups. They're a pain to schedule and I have to travel far across town for the appointment. Invariably, I have to wait or come back for a second visit. But I have regular checkups for my car because I want it to run smoothly. I don't want it to break down on the road or, worse yet, stop dead. Get the point? If I do this for my car, well . . .

Face Up. Charlie Brown was right. Face it, there are going to be ups and downs, good days and bad days. There will be tears and fears and cheers—sometimes all in the same twenty-four hours. We just have to make sure we are flexible enough mentally and spiritually to pick ourselves up.

While searching genealogy records, I have discovered the most heartbreaking incidents: the death of a child in a tub of water; fatal injury from the kick of a horse; a young mother buried on Christmas Day; a fire destroying a house the same day as a death in the family. St. Paul reminds us that all our sufferings and troubles are common to mankind, that we are not alone and that we can endure. The important thing, according to Rabbi Reb Nachman, is that we "never despair. It is forbidden to give up hope."

Tidy Up. Don't let things stay in the same place. Move them around. Rearranging forces you to get rid of clutter and to see your belongings in a new way. I favor the Five Year Rule, though it is difficult to enforce unless I'm in the proper mindset. If you haven't used an article of clothing, a device, or household item in the last five years, chances are you will not use it. Get rid of it, or at least allow someone else to enjoy it.

Throughout the day, I often invoke a Thirty Second Rule. I deliberately take thirty seconds (or less) to put jackets, receipts, earrings, eyeglasses, keys, or scissors in the place they go. Recalling the rule encourages me to take a half minute to drop dirty socks into the hamper or to put a plate in the dishwasher. If I apply the rule as much as a dozen times a day, it costs me a mere six minutes and makes my life a lot tidier. When dealing with paper or mail items, remember the acronym OHIO: *Only Handle It Once!*

Palm Up. When my doctor found that I had a vitamin D deficiency, she dosed me with heavy supplements. A friend advised a further remedy: "Sit in the sun for ten minutes a day with your palms up, because your body absorbs the rays better that way." I tried this and got terribly bored. With ten minutes on my hands, literally, I took to prayer—I reminded God of all the sick and troubled of my acquaintance. The other day, I even prayed for the nameless, bedraggled mother who was shuffling her three children along the sidewalk next to my deck. I now look forward to my "Palm" Beach time, though with winter coming on, I may have to transition to Florida if I want to maintain my physical and spiritual well-being.

Brighten Up. Laughter is the best medicine, a comedian once said. Doctors have proven him right, reporting that cheery people heal faster. So, yuck it up every chance you get. Dr. Ruth Westheimer, the eighty-year-old psychologist, is effervescent and chatty for yet another reason: "I must sing for my supper; that is to say, I can't just sit there, but must stir the pot and create active conversation to recompense the people who go out with me if I want them to be available the next time."

When there's no one else to talk to, talk to yourself. That might seem like a surefire way of appearing old, if not demented. But I'm not talking about meaningless babble. I'm suggesting the stern but encouraging self-talk that psychologists tell us can motivate us and brighten our outlook.

The Power of a Merry Heart

Some mornings I jump out of bed (well, not exactly jump—it's more of a swing), I look out the window, and I say excitedly, "What do you have in mind for us today, Lord?" (I know all too well the truth of the adage, "If you want to hear God laugh, just tell him *your* plans.") So I try to remain open to the possibilities the day may hold.

How I explain things to myself determines how I see situations and people throughout the day. When my inner chatter sounds like a Debbie Downer monologue, I know I'm in trouble. But, when I feed my thoughts upbeat messages, I feel far more relaxed and confident. I admire the attitude of the old man who looked into a full-length mirror and declared confidently, "They don't make mirrors like they used to."

I find that poetry, tunes, and verses of Scripture learned long ago still drift across my mind, reminding me of things that I value. Old hymns from my childhood are packed with power and poetry that still comfort and inspire me even now. When I need a laugh, there're always those amusing lines from Tennessee Williams' *Kitchen Door Blues.*

> My old lady died of a common cold.
>
> She smoked cigars and was ninety years old.
>
> She was slim as paper with the ribs of a kite,
>
> And she flew out the kitchen door one night.
>
> Now I'm no younger'n the old lady was,
>
> When she lost gravitation, and I smoke cigars.
>
> I feel sort of peaked, an' I look kinda pore,
>
> So, for God's sake, lock that kitchen door!

If there is a link between optimism and the immune system—and we are told there is—a cheery outlook may be just what we need to ward off disease and slow the aging process. Centuries ago, the writer of Proverbs felt there was such a link. He wrote: "A merry heart does good like a medicine, but a broken spirit dries the bones." Apparently, it has long been recognized that attitude can have a wholesome effect on both our physical and mental well-being.

Advanced Happiness

Each day we get to choose how we will perceive ourselves, our condition, and the world around us. I love the story of the ninety-two-year-old woman, poised and proud. Let's call her Mrs. Jones. She was always well-attired, with her hair carefully in place and her makeup neatly applied. But she was legally blind and unable to live alone. After her husband died, she prepared to enter a nursing home.

Arriving at the facility, she waited a good while in the lobby until an aide came to inform her that her room was ready. She smiled sweetly, thanked the young woman, and with the help of her walker started down the hall.

On the way, the aide described the layout and color scheme of the modest, little room that would be Mrs. Jones' new home.

Her face lit up. "I love it!" she stated with the glee of a child receiving a new puppy.

"But Mrs. Jones, you haven't seen the room yet. How do you know you will like it?" the aide replied.

"Whether I like my room or not doesn't depend on how the furniture is arranged . . . it's how I arrange my mind," she said. "I have already decided to love it.

"You see, every morning I wake up, I have a choice. I can spend the day in bed recounting the difficulty I have with the parts of my body that no longer work. Or, I can get out of bed and be thankful for the ones that do. Happiness is something I decide on ahead of time."

Defiant Attitude

I first read the poem "Just for Today" in an Ann Landers column many years ago. It was written by Sybyl F. Partridge in 1916 and has since been reprinted in many variations. I prefer this version because it seems so right for me. I still get a quick mental pick-me-up each time I read it.

> ### Just for Today
> I will live through the next twelve hours and not tackle my whole life's problems at once.
>
> I will improve my mind. I will learn something useful. I will read something that requires effort, thought, and consideration.
>
> I will be agreeable. I will look my best, speak in a well-modulated voice, be courteous and considerate.
>
> I will not find fault with a friend, relative, or colleague. I will not try to improve anyone or change anyone but myself.

I will have a program. I might not follow it exactly, but I will have it. I will save myself from two enemies: Hurry and Indecision.

I will exercise my character in this way: I will do a good turn and keep it secret. If anyone finds out about it, it won't count.

I will do things I don't want to do, just for exercise.

I will be unafraid, especially unafraid to enjoy what is beautiful and to believe that as I give to the world, the world will give back to me.

Not giving in to adversity or difficulty as we "mature" requires considerable grit. Overcoming obstacles—physical or mental—has always appealed to me. I recall strolling through the streets of Heidelberg, Germany, during a vacation trip. Being a camera hound, I am always on the lookout for an interesting photograph, especially one that tells a story. I saw such a picture when I spotted a single, yellow blossom growing from a rock wall that bordered the sidewalk. Like Tennyson's "crannied wall," that wall appeared to be solid, yet somehow, defiantly and against all odds, the small flower had found a crack, pushed its way toward the light and blossomed triumphantly. Now, that's what I call *attitude*. I snapped the picture and later labeled it in my album with this caption: "I, too, shall overcome."

Do the Old Rules Still Apply?

I would be remiss if I did not mention what the ancients had to say about aging. Of the Ten Commandments, the only one that comes with a promise is: "Honor thy father and mother that thy days may be long upon the earth."

We may think ancient societies went too far in revering their elderly, or even their dead ancestors, but they secured a bond at a time when survival required a strong family unit. These early families believed that a person would be treated by his own children in exactly the same manner that he treated his parents.

In a time before Social Security, Medicare, retirement homes, senior centers, home health care, and meals on wheels, it was important to establish a caring commitment to the elderly. But minister and author William Barclay cites another reason to adhere to these old rules, which is hard to ignore: "We have few duties more important than the duty of seeing that the old and the stranger are not left alone. For to them God comes in me and in you."

Today older people are less dependent on the benevolence of their offspring. Still, there is something appealing and timeless about the teachings of those musty old scrolls.

Family Secrets Are Not Just Found in the Recipes

Every family has its stories—its cast of characters, its anecdotes about what so-and-so did when, its "we used to's" (not to mention its amnesias and secrets).

—Family Secrets *by Annette Kuhn*

You might say that I had two mothers. Or so it seemed. Because Mama worked as a hairdresser much of the time, my grandmother frequently took care of me. Granny was not especially active. Her disdain for exercise or exertion, in any form, made her the perfect candidate for all sorts of ailments. Yet she was quite hearty, even though her only workout was the miles she logged in on a well-worn high-backed rocker. She hummed a lot—usually old hymns—as she swayed to and fro, day after day, mile after mile.

Granny never revealed her age, mainly because no one had ever told her exactly when she arrived. If she had any hint, she kept it to herself, leaving the rest of us to guess—and her to deny whatever number was tossed out.

"You don't know how old I am. I don't know myself," she would say trying to end the discussion.

Her age was a shifting number on which we never settled with any certainty. But even allowing for a margin of error, she lived to be at least ninety-three. I've tried to determine what contributed to her longevity.

Hymn humming? Well . . . probably not, though it undoubtedly was soothing.

Diet? Maybe.

At age forty-something, Granny learned that she had high blood pressure and should abstain from salt. After that, she never ate another potato chip or slice of ham.

Unlike my mother, a bountiful Southern cook, Granny stayed out of the kitchen. Mealtime with her was not impressive. Shredded wheat biscuits softened with hot water started the day. Lunch was often no more than a fried egg or a slice of scrapple and corn cakes made of meal and water—no salt. Dinner might be a lamb chop and greens that had been cooking all day with a piece of fatback for flavor and, of course, more corn cakes. No dessert, except fruit or a few graham crackers washed down with tea. Cups and cups of tea and salt-free crackers.

Granny avoided drafty rooms. The faintest breeze brushing against an open window would send her scurrying for a seat elsewhere. To be on the safe side, she wore a light sweater nearly all year round. In the winter, she maintained good health by avoiding crowded rooms. Overnight visits were postponed because "changing beds" would almost certainly bring on influenza, or at least a chest cold, the remedy for which was a good shellacking with Vicks salve. If that failed, a stiff shot of whiskey, (kept well-hidden for such occasions), mixed with sugar and water, produced a cure—or at least made the suffering more tolerable. (Spirits were otherwise forbidden in my family, an absence that my grandfather often remedied with a stop at the neighborhood saloon.)

Next to rocking and health care, Granny loved a Sunday afternoon ride in the country. For such occasions, my father lovingly polished the Merry Oldsmobile, bringing it to a high luster both on the outside and under the hood. He whisked the upholstery at any sign of lint. After much preparation, my grandmother would emerge from her bedroom looking for all the world like a *grande dame* on an outing along the

Champs Elysée. On these occasions, she always wore her Sunday best, set off with a two-strand pearl necklace from Palais Royale department store, white cotton gloves, a well-flowered hat with a veil, and a splash of perfume. The ubiquitous laced corset resembled plate armor and gave her a well-structured look from the waist down.

Despite the temperature, the car windows were cracked only enough to prevent the family from being overcome by heat—or the scent of perfume. My father, mother, and I sweltered, but we honored Granny's wishes, knowing that it was better to suffer some temporary discomfort than to bear the blame for causing whatever aches or pains might occur the following week. All these efforts must have had some salubrious effects, for I can never remember Granny being ill.

The Bosom Bank

My grandfather couldn't resist a gathering of his coworkers at the local saloon on payday and would occasionally come staggering along the sidewalk, winding his way home on foot. Fortunately, whether tipsy or sober, he was good-natured and soft-spoken.

Arriving home, he would slump into his easy chair and fall asleep, but not before my grandmother gave him a tongue-lashing for his waywardness. She added more guilt by rifling his pockets, removing the remainder of his pay before he awoke. The next day she would pounce on him for having lost his entire week's earnings.

Meanwhile, she had secured the hard-earned dollars in a small cloth bag with a drawstring that she kept securely pinned to the inside of her brassiere. No bank account. No sugar bowl. Just the safety of her ample bosom.

As a little girl, I can remember her giving me one of those well-protected bills for a birthday or other special occasion. The bills had a faint odor of sweat and were so tightly rolled that it was nearly impossible to flatten them out in a wallet. I would run a hot iron over my new dollar and spend it quickly. The Bosom Bank was her best-kept secret—or so I thought at the time. As far as I know, Granddaddy never figured out the scam. After all, she kept food on the table and paid the rent, skills that he happily attributed to her good management.

Strong-willed and Superstitious

My Granny, a member of the Armstrong clan, was one of seven children whose roots went back to the 18th-century Scotch-Irish settlement in Virginia. Those early settlers were a hearty breed who tamed the frontier and contributed a large part to what we call the American spirit. They were typically clannish, independent, superstitious, deeply religious, and strong-willed. But most important, they were adaptive—a necessary trait for enduring the hardships of pioneer life.

Those hearty survivalists had the stamina to stave off disease and starvation and go eye to eye with the American Indians. When tribesmen came after them with tomahawks, the Scotch-Irish retaliated in kind and displaced a few scalps themselves. Happily, they made their peace with the Native Americans and produced some descendents, giving me the opportunity to be a card-carrying member of the Patawomeck Indian tribe.

Although no violence was evident in the family in my day, Granny could still carry a grudge with the best. She remembered clearly that Mrs. Newton had failed to speak to her at the grocery store one day twenty years earlier. Her superstitions were real, too, having been implanted years ago, and no scientific evidence to the contrary could alter them. As a child, I can remember her stern admonitions.

"Don't rock that chair with no one in it," she'd caution.

"Why not?" I would ask tauntingly. "What's wrong with rocking a chair?"

"Just don't you do it. You never know what might happen."

She never said exactly. It was almost as though the curse was too horrible to reveal. I suspect it had something to do with death, but she never said for sure.

To Granny, thunderstorms were the "Lord's work," and an activity to be revered. My cousins and I had to refrain from rowdy games or loud talking and remain respectfully solemn during such times. Ill omens also surround Friday, and nothing of importance was commenced on such an inauspicious day.

Sunday, too, had its special requirements. A needle and thread were never used on the Lord's Day, even if a button fell from the dress you were about to wear to church. The garment was changed and the repair work delayed until the next day.

Responsibility had befallen my grandmother in her preteen years. After her mother died, she was left with the care of the younger children while her father, a tenant farmer, and the boys worked the fields. One of her vivid recollections was of fleeing the house to get away from the overwhelming task, only to run into an apparition of her mother standing in the doorway and insisting that she return. It was enough of a scare to keep her on the job for a few more years.

I realize now that it was not Granny's intention to teach me error. It was just that her mind brimmed with misinformation gleaned over the years and guarded tenaciously against anything to the contrary. Because she had only a few years of schooling and little exposure to the outside world, opportunity had passed her by, just as it had for so many women of her era. She never held a job, owned a home, or voted; never drove a car or traveled by train or airplane; never visited a museum or art gallery or attended a play; and never wrote a check.

Her Really *Big* Secret

The summer I was ten years old, my mother began working in the government in Washington, D.C. It was the patriotic thing to do. World War II was in full sway. It became my responsibility to accompany my grandmother to the grocery store, a task that led me to discover her well-kept secret.

Since Granny didn't drive, we walked the six blocks to the Acme Grocery each week. I still remember how much I disliked that task. But one day as we arrived at the store, I looked down the street and saw a man on a ladder painting letters on a plate-glass window. The outline read PUBLIC LIBRARY NOW OPEN.

I was so excited!

I said, "Granny, is it all right if I go to the new library while you shop? I'll be right there to help with the grocery bags when you get through."

She reluctantly agreed. For the next half hour, I was in heaven surrounded by all those wonderful books—more books than I had ever seen in my life. I always felt like a misfit in a family that valued work more than words. There were no books in my home, not even a dictionary, unless you counted the Bible and the musty set of Colliers encyclopedias that filled a small bookshelf in the living room.

In a transcendent state, surrounded by hundreds of books, I forgot all about Granny and the groceries. A pecking on the windowpane jarred me back to my real world. I looked up. There was my grandmother making beckoning motions for me to come help her with the groceries.

I quickly checked out three books, and we juggled books and bags all the way home. I spent the next week—every chance I got—with my newfound treasures. It was a hot, humid summer, before the days of air conditioning, so I spent much of the time on the front porch of our row house. Sitting in the squeaky glider with a flyswatter and a glass of Kool-Aid nearby, I was in another world.

By the next week, I had finished my reading and was looking forward to the grocery-shopping trip and the chance to acquire more books.

As time went on, however, it troubled me that my grandmother showed no interest in the books that I found so compelling.

One day I said, "Granny, I wish you would read this book."

She said no, she wasn't interested.

I said, "But just read this part here. It is so good."

It was then that she told me something I couldn't believe.

She said, "I can't read."

I said, "What do you mean, you can't read? *Everybody* can read!"

She explained that, after her mother's death, there was never time for school or books. Work and daily survival mattered most. Time was wasted that did not put food on the table or hay in the barn. It was a shame she bore each day; a condition that crippled her life.

In my youthful exuberance I said, "I'll teach you! What do you want to read?"

She said she had always wanted to read the Bible. Frankly, at the time, that was not my book of choice. But we read the Bible that summer, and I suspect it did me more good than it did her. Later I joined the Dollar-a-Book Club and started getting pulp novels through the mail. After just one Frank Yerby Southern romance, Granny was hooked on reading.

More Secrets

That particular summer I learned even more family lore. Apparently, Granny had decided I was old enough to be entrusted with the "family secrets." I learned that a few generations earlier a relative, or two, had given birth "out of wedlock." A great-uncle had married a Catholic woman (which was finally forgiven him, because she turned out to be such a good wife and offered a daily novena for anyone who was sick in the family). Granny also revealed that a great-aunt had lived all her adult life with a female companion; one enterprising relative had run a whiskey still during Prohibition; and, (*gasp*), there were a couple of American Indians in the family gene pool.

Most disturbing to my Virginia ancestors was my great-grandfather, who had deserted the Southern cause because it was harvest time and he had a family to feed that winter. None of these confessions seemed as bothersome to me as they were to my grandmother. I tried not to yawn, hoping she would eventually get to the juicy parts. But that was it. Either we were a boring family, or someone had already sifted out the more salacious nuggets. Even so, I showed my appreciation for her trust by agreeing not to reveal any of these hidden tidbits to friends or neighbors. I put the stories out of mind entirely until years later, when some of the incidents popped up while I was doing genealogy research.

Every family has its ancestral cover-ups that range from the hilarious to the hurtful. Or, as the old English proverb declares, "He who has no fools, knaves, or beggars in his family was begot by a flash of lightning." In most cases, memories fade and views evolve, lessening the impact of what once seemed outrageous or shameful. No one should be held hostage by some deep, dark secret of a former generation. We may inherit the past, but we get to shape the future.

Faith

Faith is the daring of the soul to go farther than it can see.
—William Newton Clarke

You Are What You Think You Are

What you think means more than anything else in your life.
More than what you earn; more than where you live; more
than your social position, and more than what anyone else may
think about you.
—George Matthew Adams, author

I n the film *Young Frankenstein*, when Igor is asked about the foot-high hump on his back, he responds, "What hump?" We can't always control circumstances and events, but we can control our reaction to life.

A friend who recently lost her husband inquired of me, "Do people ever say to you, 'What's it like to be a widow?'" Though it's been eight years since the plane crash, I was startled to be referred to as a *widow*. I caught myself before I blurted out, "But I'm not a . . . "

Sure, I've checked those marital status boxes on printed forms, but I have never thought of myself as a widow in the traditional sense. For so long, society has identified widows as poor, sniveling souls unable to face the world. Even so, a few feisty widows make it on to the pages of the Bible (Ruth, Naomi, and the one who took on the unjust judge). In more recent literature, widows were portrayed as crotchety old women like the Widow Douglas, who tried to reform Huck Finn.

Today most widows are nothing like these stereotypes. Upon the loss of a husband, they often step up to take over major businesses, manage the family farm, go back to school, travel, or run for office. If life is like a book—as we are told it is—we should earmark or underline those wonderful portions we want to remember. But we must keep turning the pages, moving on to the next chapters to see what exciting things the Author has in store for us. We must not miss out on those last chapters, because they are so much a part of our whole story.

The Doers versus the Downers

Regardless of our age or status, most people have figured out that the world is divided into *doers* and *downers*—those who see the possibilities and those who see the gloom. One early incident that separated the two occurred shortly after a rag-tag band of slaves left Egypt, headed for the Promised Land. As they approached Canaan and thought about all the uncertainty of the future, they did what any normal group of people would do today: They formed a committee.

The committee of twelve was probably the first on record. Their assignment was to search out the new land and bring back a report on what they discovered. It took them forty days, so we know it was a thorough exploration.

Following their investigation, they were all in agreement. Well . . . at least on one point. They agreed that their new homeland was everything that God had promised; it was a land that flowed with "milk and honey." The committee brought proof of their conclusion—grape branches so heavy they had to be supported on poles carried on the men's shoulders.

That was the good news.

The bad news was that there were people living there in walled cities that were much larger and more powerful than the Israelites. Ten of the committeemen summed up the majority feeling: "We looked at those giants and we were in our sight as grasshoppers."

Overpowered by their feelings of inadequacy, they reasoned that it was better to return to slavery in Egypt than to take on such a risky venture. Only Joshua and Caleb felt a victory was possible.

"Let us go over at once and possess the land," they argued, "for we are well able to do it."

But the "downers" prevailed, and because of their faithless attitude, the Israelites were left to wander in the wilderness until that generation of unbelievers had died.

A Second Chance

The next time the wanderers approached Canaan, Caleb was eighty-five years old. At that age, you would think that his vigor might have diminished. Instead, Caleb told the people that he felt as fit as ever. Neither his strength nor enthusiasm had waned during the past forty-some years. As the land was being divided, Caleb didn't ask for a prime location, which he most certainly deserved. Instead, he pointed toward Mount Hebron and said, "Give me this mountain."

The rest of the verse tells us that the hilly region was inhabited by giants. Those same fearsome, oversized warriors were still there. But Caleb was undeterred. He was still looking for mountains to climb and giants to overcome. Caleb reminds us, as George Eliot would centuries later, that "you are never too old to be what you might have been."

Dreamers Conquer Mountains

I have discovered that—for better or worse—I am part of a family of dreamers. I was reminded of that when I met a woman who had known the Carnahan family years ago. She told of cleaning out a dresser drawer and finding a 1934 high school graduation program that showed my father-in-law, A. S. J. Carnahan, was the commencement speaker. She thought our family would want to have it.

As I examined the yellowed leaflet, I recalled that during the thirties, our country was struggling to pull out of the Great Depression—a time of widespread hopelessness and economic despair. My father-in-law, a rural school teacher, was being paid in warrants, which were just promises to pay if money became available. Those government IOUs didn't put food on the table, but they were better than nothing.

I looked to see what he had spoken about during such hard times. The title of his commencement address was *Climb Though the Road Seems Rugged*. I had to laugh, because that theme could have been the motto for his life. He was the last of ten children, born in a poor Ozark community and the only one in his family to get a college education. While his siblings all bore the names of Biblical heroes, he was tagged with the name of a hapless Confederate general, Albert Sidney Johnston, and even that was misspelled. But he had dreams, though there was no reason to believe they would ever come true.

Ten years after that speech, he came home one evening and made a shocking announcement. He told his family that he was going to run for Congress.

His wife said, "Don't do it; you can't win."

He told his friends and neighbors.

They said, "Don't do it; you can't win."

He told the local politicians.

They said, "Don't do it; you can't win."

Well, he ran anyway.

And you know, they were right. He didn't win.

But he wasn't defeated. Personally, that is. That's what made the difference.

He ran again in the next election. That time he won, and he went on winning for six more terms. He later became a delegate to the United Nations and ended his career in government as an ambassador to Sierra Leone. Some forty years later, my son, Russ, would run for that same congressional seat. Like his grandfather, he lost, but with the same indomitable spirit, he ran again, this time in St. Louis among a field of ten candidates and won.

When people comment on our family's political inclination, I refer to it—only somewhat jokingly—as a genetic defect.

The Risk of Trying

My family endures my corny jokes, even when they are at their expense. I call my youngest son, Tom, a modern–day Don Quixote— the errant knight who engaged in the ludicrous practice of tilting with windmills. Tom used to ignore my description of him; now, in retrospect, he laughs—and for good reason.

In 2004, Tom became enchanted with the possibility of constructing windmills to ease the nation's energy crunch. He saw the absence of commercial turbines in Missouri as an opportunity to be explored. So great was his interest that he decided to give up his law practice to become a "wind farmer." The few people he told about his decision laughed at him.

Because chasing the wind seemed so absurd, he quietly pursued his goal without discussing it with family or friends. He discovered that the windiest parts of Missouri are in the northwest, where many small towns are in transition. They were once thriving communities, but today there are fewer residents, less revenue for schools and services, and little hope for the future.

But they still have the wind, a great source of alternative energy. Today, because of Tom's dreams, there are eighty 200-ton turbines sitting in plowed fields scattered across northwest Missouri—and more on the way. Like giant sculptures, they are designed to spin against the sky, their blades stretching the length of a football field.

Harvesting the wind provides farmers with an additional cash crop while their communities profit from an increased tax base. The local electrical cooperatives benefit also, as do consumers who gain a new, green energy supply. Their ability to capture the wind has transformed these communities and brightened their futures. It started when one person believed it could be done. Carl Sandburg was right: "Nothing happens until first a dream."

Ten Times Thirty

I am grateful for those YOU ARE HERE maps at the shopping malls. With little effort, I can chart the most direct course to where I want to go. I wish all of life's pathways were so clearly mapped, color coded, and written in large print for our convenience. But they are not.

When we are looking for direction and nothing seems obvious, we are left to rely on our faith. If we take the first step toward our goal—no matter how small or insignificant that stride might be—the next step becomes easier and more apparent. From our new vantage point, things look differently. What once seemed unattainable when we were frozen by fear and confusion suddenly seems possible.

Some years ago, a group of airmen, who could barely walk, put their faith to the test. It was during World War II; their bomber had been shot down in the Burmese jungle. By some miracle, the men onboard survived, but many of them were injured. They looked at their map and discovered they were three hundred miles from an American base.

The men were completely disheartened. There was no way they could walk that far through jungles, over mountainous terrain, through the rain and heat, back to their base. They knew where they wanted to go, but they had little hope of ever getting there.

The captain knew he was going to have to do something or they would die there in the jungle. He discovered from the map that the villages were about ten miles apart.

So he asked, "How many of you think you can walk ten miles?"

They all agreed they might be able to walk that distance. And they did.

The next day he asked, "How many think you can walk ten miles today?" Again, they all agreed they'd give it a try. So, day by day, they kept walking, until they finally made it back to safety.

The captain was later interviewed by a reporter, who asked: "Under such hopeless circumstances, with that terrible terrain, and with all those wounded, dispirited men, how were you able to walk three hundred miles back to your base?"

The officer replied, "Oh, we never walked three hundred miles. We could never have done that. We just walked ten miles, thirty times."

Reaching our goal is seldom accomplished with a giant leap. It's more a series of little steps moving in the right direction that finally gets us where we want to be. It all begins in our thoughts. We have to believe we can accomplish something, before we can do it.

Thoughts Reign

Writers, philosophers, and teachers over the centuries have come to a common conclusion: "We are what we think about all day." Henry Thoreau made a daily practice of repeating to himself all the good news he could think of. By doing so, he was able to override any pessimism that crept into his thinking.

We were not made to be like grasshoppers, fearful and small. If the story of Joshua and Caleb teaches us anything, it is that we are conquerors able to overcome gigantic obstacles. In both body and spirit, we are designed to scale the mountains, not to wander aimlessly in the wilderness.

The World Is a
Very Narrow Bridge

*It helps, I think, to consider ourselves on a very long journey: the
main thing is to keep to the faith, to endure, to help each other
when we stumble or tire, to weep and press on.*
—Mary Caroline Richards, poet

S ome years ago while traveling in Taiwan, I crossed a bridge—a rope
footbridge—leading to a monastery. At first I wasn't quite sure that
I wanted to make the crossing. The flimsy bridge overlooked menacing
rapids that pounded on the huge rocks jutting from the river.

All I could think of was the old joke about the man who was considering such a crossing, when he noticed that one of the ropes on the footbridge was frayed.

He asked the monk giving the tour, "How often do you replace the ropes?"

The monk replied, "Every time they break."

But Rabbi Nachman didn't see it that way. Years ago, he declared that we should be there for one another before tragedy strikes. One version of his well-known verse goes: "All of the world is a very narrow bridge . . . and the main thing is, though we fear, we won't let each other fall." His words of caution are not just about maintaining our foothold on the bridge, but in seeing that those around us don't slip. I think that's what the Founding Fathers had in mind, too, when they wrote about us looking out for the "general welfare" and securing the "blessings of liberty."

The Ropes are Fraying and Breaking

For some, a helping hand or a verbal pat on the back is all they need to get across the bridge that marks our common journey. Others need more dramatic assistance.

When I was in the U. S. Senate, I met Dr. Barbara Ehrenreich, a social commentator in her late fifties, author of *Nickel and Dimed in*

America. To write her story, she went undercover for two years to find out what it was like to live among the working poor. She took a series of jobs, ranging from hotel maid to nursing home assistant to Wal-Mart clerk, and lived on the salaries.

I said to her, "No matter how hard you tried, there was a difference between you and your coworkers. You knew that at the end of two years, things would change. You had hope. What would you have done if you did not have that hope?"

She replied in all seriousness, "I would have found a bridge somewhere and jumped off."

Ehrenreich's story shows how removed we are from the feelings and frustration of those who live hand-to-mouth. It has become increasingly acceptable to ignore the chronically poor or to blame them for their plight. Most of us are safely walled off from contact with the destitute. They don't live in our neighborhoods or play with our children. They are not in our work places. They don't attend our churches or social events. They don't vacation in the same places or shop in the same stores. Most often the poor are faceless—a statistic that we hear reported once a year.

Perhaps that's why the events of Hurricane Katrina were especially alarming. Thousands of helpless people were thrust into our living rooms each evening as their tragedies unfolded before our eyes on national television. We were very uncomfortable seeing the real trap of poverty. We watched the bridge we share become a lot narrower and the journey more hazardous for all of us.

The Faces of Poverty

I never come upon a homeless person without thinking of that conversation between a shopkeeper and beggar in *Fiddler on the Roof.* The shopkeeper puts a coin in the beggar's cup; the beggar is disgruntled. He reaches into the cup, retrieves the coin, looks up at the shopkeeper and says, "Can't you do better?"

The shopkeeper replies, "I had a bad year," to which the beggar replies, "Because you had a bad year, I should suffer?"

I know that the solution to poverty in America is more than dropping a few coins in the hat of a homeless person. Yet in recent years, I have begun giving to those begging along the streets or standing in the median at the traffic lights. I can think of dozens of reasons why I shouldn't. I didn't used to give them anything. I was more comfortable giving to the local food pantry or the Salvation Army. Since the Katrina floods, I feel the face-to-face encounter with a struggling human being requires some response on my part.

I can't believe that the shabby guy with the icicles in his beard, holding a cardboard sign reading NEED FOOD, has deliberately chosen this activity as his life's work. Or that he has parlayed his panhandling into an enormous Swiss bank account.

When I do give a few dollars on the street, invariably the person with me says, "Why did you do that? They're just going to spend it on booze or cigarettes."

"Maybe," I say, "but maybe not."

The Narrow Bridge to the Global Village

My first grade reading book was entitled *Friendly Village*. The quaint neighborhood featured Dick, Jane, Sally, Spot, and Puff. In Friendly Village, there were no crimes, poverty, unemployment, or graffiti. It was a charming place, isolated and idyllic.

In Friendly Village, violence was no more than Spot chasing Puff across the lawn. The only tears shed occurred when Jane scratched her knee falling from a scooter. Meals in Friendly Village were hearty and healthful and in a home that included a well-dressed family, a father with a job, a mother who stayed home to cook and clean, and children who attended school.

Today's village is more global and its makeup far more diverse. Its problems are troubling and the residents not always friendly. To sense the true makeup of the world, analysts suggest that we shrink the earth's population to a village of precisely one hundred people, with the human ratios remaining the same. According to the 100 People Foundation, in the Global Village at the turn of the 21st century there would be:

- 61 Asians, 12 Europeans, 14 from the Western Hemisphere (North and South), and 13 Africans
- 50 would be female; 50 would be male
- 80 would be non-white; 20 white
- 69 would be non-Christian; 31 Christian
- 20 people would earn 89 percent of the entire village's wealth
- 25 would live in substandard housing
- 18 would be unable to read
- 17 would suffer from malnutrition
- 1 would be near death; 1 would be near birth
- Only 1 would have a college education
- 1 would own a computer

The Real Village of the World

Nearly three billion people (half the world) live on less than two dollars a day—the bare subsistence level. Thirty thousand children die each day from lack of food, clean drinking water, or immunizations that would have saved their lives. One billion people entered the 21st century unable to read a book or sign their name.

What must be done? The answer is as old as the question.

Centuries ago, Isaiah called upon us to be the " . . . repairer of the breach, the restorer of paths." Isaiah's concept is embodied in the ancient Jewish teaching known as *tikkun olam*. It means *repairing the world—* that is, taking responsibility for correcting the damage done by people to each other, as well as to the planet.

I like to think that if we can mend a moment in time, perhaps we can mend a millennium. At least, we must try. For our own well-being— if for no other reason—we must find new ways to make our "village" friendly.

No Way Out

The oldest of writings tell us that we cannot love God and ignore poverty, injustice, and mercy. The Bible alone has more than two thousand verses about the poor. Poverty is not mentioned in the Ten Commandments, but Moses later issued some stern requirements: " . . . do not be hardhearted or tightfisted toward your poor brother. Give generously to him and do so without a grudging heart; then because of this the Lord your God will bless you in all your work and in everything you put your hand to."

Jesus further personalized the issue, telling us that whatever we do for others, we do for Him. The Apostle John picked up the theme when he posed the haunting question: "If I see a brother in need and do not do something about it, how can the love of God exist in me?"

The saints, from Francis of Assisi to Mother Teresa, felt like God somehow dwelled within the poor in a way that requires our attention. Kagawa, the Japanese Christian, writing of poverty in his country during the early 20th century, went so far as to say that if we fail to see God in the human face, we will never see Him.

Neither Moses, Jesus, St. Francis, Mother Teresa nor Kagawa gives us a way out. They do not require that the poor be deserving, clean, grateful or godly in order to qualify for our benevolence. If God resides with the poor, the hurting, and the powerless, how can we know Him, if we are searching elsewhere?

We shirk our duty to the poor at our own peril.

Encouragement Lifts the Heart

*Treat people as if they were who they ought to be and you help
them to become what they are capable of being.*

—Goethe

Much of what we need to know in life comes from learning the hard way. You don't even remember one of the earliest of your experiences in this School of Hard Knocks. But your parents and relatives do.

It was your first steps.

I suspect you were cautious about stepping out. You had never done anything like that before.

But there were people there urging you on.

Smiling.

Reaching out to you.

Telling you that you could do it.

You were thinking, *Should I believe them?*

Should I let go of the coffee table?

And finally, you did something that was very instinctive. You trusted those who loved you. You let go.

You took a step . . . and another . . . and another.

You were beaming and feeling so good.

Then something happened . . . and you fell flat on your . . . *diaper!*

You began to whimper.

What happened? I was doing so well.

About that time, a sea of hands reached out to you and lifted you onto your feet again. As they soothed you with words of praise and encouragement, you thought to yourself, *Life is going to be a piece of cake. All I have to do is take some baby steps and everyone will cheer me on.*

Then fear struck . . . fear of failure.

But somewhere down inside you mustered the courage to try again, and with each step you felt stronger and more confident.

If our first steps taught us anything, it was that life was going to be a series of downs and ups, failures and recoveries, tears and triumphs. Those early feelings have been repeated many times. We have all felt lonely, frightened at the next step, doubtful of ourselves and others.

Fortunately, there are those along the way to cheer us on.

The Boost of Encouragement

How thankful I am for Encouragers—those sensitive souls who add joy to our lives and lessen our sorrows. They add quality to life and soften the blows. When we meet these people, we are immediately attracted to them. They are easily recognized, for there is an essence about them that pervades everything they do.

We are never too young or too old, too important or too insignificant to need the reassurance of others. All of us benefit from a morale boost, especially when we become discouraged, overwhelmed, or apprehensive. I admire the elderly volunteer who confessed with a twinkle in his eye, "I try to do something good for someone everyday without getting caught."

The transforming power of encouragement and belief is key to Cervantes' classical tale of Don Quixote, a 16th-century knight on a ridiculous quest to conquer a mixed-up world. Being part of a family that has pursued a number of seemingly impossible ventures, I feel enough in common with the fictitious knight to keep a collection of Quixote figures on my bookshelf.

The theme of the story is recounted in the play *The Man of La Mancha*, and the song "The Impossible Dream," in which the errant knight refuses to see the world as it is, but perceives it—and people—as they could be. In his pursuits, he meets a local bar maid with a poor reputation, but he treats her with great respect, dubbing her his Lady Dulcinea. Because of his belief that she was something more, she becomes a changed person. On his deathbed, she comes in. When he asks who it is, she responds, "I am your Lady Dulcinea." His belief in her had been transforming.

Try Giving Yourself Away

As a teenager, I came upon a fascinating idea when I read the book *Try Giving Yourself Away* by David Dunn. It was one of the many volumes I lost in my house fire several years ago, but have since found on eBay. The author had an unusual hobby. He gave away something each day that benefited others but cost him little or nothing. Actually, it was like a "reverse hobby," he said. Some people collect or acquire; he saw himself as a resource to be given away.

Dunn was sensitive to the timing of his deeds. His awareness allowed him to find everyday opportunities to show appreciation, gratitude, sympathy, enthusiasm, forgiveness, praise, and encouragement. Giving a smile or a compliment, remembering a birthday with a note or phone call added to his pleasure and that of others. Dunn kept no daily record of his deeds, nor did he expect to be repaid for his goodness. He felt that these contributions to life were of no value unless they were given away.

Immediate Job Openings

As I grow older (Oops! I mean *mature*), I have discovered a wonderful career opportunity as an Encourager. The work is fascinating, but it has required me to brush up on my awareness and sensitivity. Compensation is proportionate to the effort expended, and there is definitely opportunity for advancement.

In my latest vocation as an Encourager, I get to point out to my kids, grandkids, friends, public servants, store clerks, and total strangers, something they have done right. This sometimes takes effort, but I am improving. Watch out, because I am armed! I am armed with hugs, smiles, back pats, hand squeezes, and lifted thumbs, and I am not afraid to use them.

In my mind, I sometimes wear the uniform of a perky, young cheerleader with a big *E* on my sweater. With megaphone hoisted, I am single-handedly rooting a dispirited quarterback down the field. Other times, I slip into the outfit of a caped crusader, fighting for hope, courage, and the optimistic way of life.

I have found work in the encouragement field to be satisfying, steady, and rewarding, and the opportunities are unparalleled. For those who are interested, immediate openings are available in most locations.

Encouraging Results

I have also become a collector of encouraging stories, some serious and others amusing, as is this one about Richard Nixon. His staff recognized that their boss was not an especially talented debater. Still, they wanted to do all they could to encourage him and to keep him feeling good about his performance. Prior to one political debate, without Nixon's knowledge, they hired an elderly woman to attend and hold a big campaign sign. After the event, she was to come up to Nixon and say something positive and encouraging about his performance.

As expected, Nixon did not do very well in that debate. As he came off the platform, he saw this woman smiling broadly and waving his campaign sign. So, he just naturally gravitated that way. As he reached out to her, she understood her job. She grabbed Nixon by the hand and said warmly, "Don't you worry none, Mr. President, you'll do better next time."

If we fail, how wonderful it is to have someone ready to give us a lift, to remind us that we "can do better next time."

Heavyweight boxing champion Muhammad Ali had his own professional Encourager, his corner man and assistant trainer Drew "Bundini" Brown. After retiring, Brown wrote the book, *You Gotta Believe*, telling how he used positive phrases to help the shy prizefighter gain the confidence he needed to win.

Among Ali's more memorable lines were "I'm the greatest" and "Float like a butterfly, sting like a bee." Ali knew that no matter how much he was hurting or inclined to give up, Bundini would be in his corner waiting to cheer him on for another round.

Not all Encouragers are professional. Writer Martha Baker told of guiding mothers, which she identified as "any older woman who offers help or inspires others."

"I just want someone older to recognize me, to ask about my work," she wrote. "Someone happy to hug me with arms or words." Yes, we all need to be hugged with arms and words.

The Secret of Happiness

Stories of Encouragers abound in the folklore of all cultures. I once read an Irish folktale about a little girl playing in a field outside her village. She comes upon a butterfly impaled by a thorn on a fence post.

She feels so saddened by the sight, that she gently removes the thorn. When she does, the butterfly immediately turns into a leprechaun. The leprechaun is so touched by her kindness that he offers to grant her any wish.

The little girl declares, "I want to always be happy."

Whereupon, the leprechaun whispers a few words in her ear and disappears. After that, she was the happiest person in the village. She was often asked what caused her to be such a happy person.

She would always reply, "Oh, it's a lesson I learned from the leprechaun."

Finally, as she grew old and was on her deathbed, the villagers gathered around to pay their final respects.

Not wanting the secret of happiness to die with her, they pleaded with her, "Tell us the secret of the leprechaun."

She said, "Oh, it was all so simple, just three words. He said to me, 'Everybody needs you.'"

Imagine living each day as though you were needed by everyone you met. When we think of ourselves as an answer, a lifter, or an encourager, we have the power to change any situation.

Fortunately, Encouragers are a genus of humankind scattered throughout civilization. Centuries ago, Eliphaz consoled Job, his distraught friend, telling him, "Your words have kept men on their feet."

Isaiah painted a beautiful word picture of the Encourager. He wrote: "For you have been a defense for the helpless . . . a refuge from the storm, a shade from the heat."

When looking for opportunities to be an Encourager, this simple Buddhist prayer is a good one to remember.

May I become at all times,

Both now and forever,

A protector for the helpless,

A guide for the lost ones,

A ship for those to cross oceans,

And a bridge to cross rivers,

A sanctuary for those in danger,

A lamp for those in darkness,

A refuge for those who lack shelter,

And a servant to all in need.

God Works in Wondrous Ways

*It becomes very obvious that God is everywhere and in everything
and we cannot be without Him.*

—Thomas Merton

As I write these words, I am sitting on a beach in San Juan, Puerto Rico, looking out onto the ocean. Frankly, I don't do my best writing in the tropics. I am distracted by the brisk breezes, frolicking children, sunbathers, and the daredevil antics of surfers.

Even so, on family holidays such as this, I don a floppy hat and squeeze into a bathing suit long since out of style and a bit snug. I dutifully put on a pair of flip-flops that I reserve for such occasions.

They are always uncomfortable because feet my age rebel at having a spacer between the toes.

I note that my frayed beach bag still has several tablespoons of sand left over from a previous vacation. Without removing the sand, I stuff the bag with the day's essentials: number 45 sun screen, room keys, wallet, sunglasses, reading glasses, the day's newspaper, towel, cell phone, comb, Chapstick, long sleeve shirt, camera, and a few books and pieces of fruit. The handles of the bag barely meet as I insert yet another item: a note pad on which to pencil any random thoughts.

I am ready for a day at the seashore.

The truth is, I don't care much for water—unless it's in a Jacuzzi. During our family outings on the Eastern shore, I was content to squish about the water's edge while pondering the discarded shells of former lives that lay along the beach. As the tide tugged at my feet, I would fight back, not daring to give up control to the undertow.

Now, as I lumber across the sand, I feel as out of my element as a beached manatee. Arriving at the spot I had selected the previous day, I discover it is occupied by a young woman who has already staked her claim and slaked her body with lotion, and is now in the process of attaching herself to an iPod.

I move farther down the shoreline and establish my new beachhead near a family building a sandcastle with a moat. Standing at the water's edge is a handsome, well-tanned instructor giving a lesson on kite boarding. The couple tries to manipulate the arc-shaped kite strapped to their bodies while attempting to ride a surfboard. It seems a lot like patting your head and rubbing your stomach at the same time. They are slow to learn the technique and spend a lot of time bobbing in the water.

Despite the sand in my crevices, wind in my hair, and sun in my eyes, I try to prepare myself for what Wordsworth called the "joy of elevated thoughts." But as I engage in a battle of wills with my lounge chair, all I can think of is that exchange between Lucy and Charlie Brown. From her psychiatric booth, she tells him, "Life is like a deck chair on the cruise ship of life; some people place their deck chair at the rear of the ship so they can see where they've been. Others place their deck chair at the front of the ship so they can see where they're going. Which way is your deck chair facing, Charlie Brown?" Charlie replies glumly, "I can't even get my deck chair unfolded."

I eventually win the lounge-chair struggle with only a pinched finger. As I settle in, I attempt to reclaim my thoughts. I recall Anne Morrow Lindberg's seaside reverie in *Gift from the Sea*, a smallish book that I have read on previous beach vacations. "Patience and faith," I repeated to myself—that's what she said we learn from the sea.

I put her theory to the test, by closing my eyes and taking some deep, relaxing breaths. But, again, my thoughts wander.

Have I put enough sunscreen on my legs?

Probably not.

I drag my beach bag toward me and locate the lotion, which has already found its way to the bottom of the bag. While I'm there, I check my phone for e-mail messages and apply some Chapstick.

I settle back to enjoy my "kingdom by the sea."

The Tide Always Comes Back

Within minutes, my mind is caught up in the pounding of the waves that lash the shore in a rhythmic fashion, as they have since the beginning of time. I have come to appreciate the magnitude of the ocean with its tides so predictable that we can chart the exact time of their highs and lows.

I listen for the near silence that comes between the ebb and flow of the waves. Lindberg called it "the pause that occurs between when a wave extends to its fullest on the beach and retreats to flow back into the ocean." It reminded her of the need to pause, to reflect, and to gain the strength that hurried women require.

I think to myself: I was once a "hurried" woman eager to accomplish new tasks and explore places unknown. Now, all that remain are my hurried thoughts. My mind wants to flow, while my body prefers to ebb.

Down the beach, I spot a dingy partially buried in the sand. It looks much like a lithograph I once saw of an old boat stranded on the shore when the tide went out. The boat is stuck, useless—unable to go anyplace. The title of the image was *The Tide Always Comes Back*. What a wondrous assurance! When the tide returns—as it most surely will— the boat will be lifted to dance over the waves as it was meant to do. In the ebb and flow of life, we sometimes feel beached and hopeless. But in time, God's goodness washes over us, and we are afloat again, buoyed by His grace.

Though I love the sand and surf, I have concluded that I am not a natural beach body. My skin is far too fair and requires lotions and cover-ups. My hair is inclined to frizz in humid weather, my feet are too tender from being encased in socks and shoes, and my physique is not suited for public display.

Yet, I come back to the seashore year after year. I am attracted by the tides that splash persistently onto the shore. I feel some kinship with this untamed force that lunges onto the beach, then retreats to familiar waters to gather strength. There is a lesson to be learned from the waves as they pound the shore with such self-abandon: Life is not always about success; it's more about mighty endeavor.

Staying in Tune

I don't need to be surrounded by magnificent seashores, rugged mountain peaks, or breathtaking vistas to be reminded of God's presence in the world. I find evidence of Him in ordinary things, in strange places, and where I least expect. John Wheelwright, the poet, wrote: "Cleave a seed—I am there; split the rock, you shall find me." Ralph Waldo Emerson had similar thoughts. He wrote, "All of life is a miracle from the blowing clover to the falling rain."

With that in mind, I look for occurrences of wonder in nature and in commonplace events. One took place along the dirt road that runs in front of my farm house. I used to run a mile and a half to the end of the road and back: a three-mile workout. I seldom saw a car, and there were few houses. My only amusement was in seeing an occasional flock of turkeys or a deer sprinting across an open field. Sometimes a turtle crossing the road would pause mid-way until I had passed. A jog along County Road 4040 meant encountering the ordinary, not the amazing. That's why it was such a wonderful path for reflection.

One day I came upon an eerie scene. It was October, and the air was brisk. Falling leaves spun about in the breeze forming a kaleidoscope of color as they floated earthward. Surely it was on such a day that Edna St. Vincent Millay wrote, "Lord, I do fear thou'st made the world too beautiful this year."

As I huffed up the hill to my turn-around point, I noticed a single leaf dancing several feet in the air, as though magically suspended in space. All around other leaves were drifting downward, but not this one. What would cause such an oddity?

I approached cautiously and was about to pass my hand above the leaf to test whatever connection was causing it to hover in space. But my hand stopped short when I saw a thin, nearly invisible cobweb. The web had caught the leaf, breaking its fall.

The presence of the unseen thread at just the right moment was enough to support the falling leaf in the blustery wind. We, too, are held tenderly and invisibly by God's grace. His assurance to Abraham is ours as well: "I am your refuge and strength and underneath are the everlasting arms." When we trip on the loose stones of life, how wonderful it is to know that we fall into the arms of a loving God.

Inexplicable Wonder

I love waking up to the gentle rumble of thunder. No loud claps or frightening zaps of lightning, just soft, non-threatening grumbles, as though God is bowling a gutter ball instead of a strike. I know a young mother who tells her frightened children that thunder is God clapping his hands. My grandmother would have thought such analogies over-familiar, if not sacrilegious. She considered a thunderstorm "the Lord's work" and a time when we children had to refrain from rowdy games and remain respectful of the heavenly display. I still think about her admonitions during turbulent weather, though even as a child I took exception to her theology. My complaint was that it emphasized a Thor-like deity up there, far away, rather than a caring God beside me, here and now.

Granny held some firm ideas about the source of lightning, too. It was the finger of God, zapping across the sky, touching down where it may. I tried to explain that it came from electrical charges that build up inside a storm cloud, the protons, or positive atoms, at the top and the electrons, or negative atoms, on the bottom. When these atoms get too crowded they jump to another area of the cloud or to the ground, creating a huge spark of static electricity. To Granny, such thinking was the "invention of the Devil" and best put out of mind.

Despite her dire warnings, the more I learned, the more I marveled at the universe and our capacity to thrive on this little orb we call Earth. Our living here depends on so many cosmic details being just right. Earth is like the porridge in the story of the three bears; it can't be too cold or too hot. We are just the right distance from the sun not to fry or to become icicles.

We have just the right amount of gravity and the correct balance of oxygen and water to survive. We have bodies that adapt to the most rigorous of conditions and come in more varieties than a jumbo box of Crayolas. Though we may be intrigued by the electrical system of a space ship and the complexity of the Internet, neither compares with the workings of the brain, with its millions of neurological pathways.

Within us, divine sparks of goodness ignite acts of sacrifice, empathy, faith, and mercy that separate us from other life forms. I have a hard time believing such complexity is the result of some galactic accident. Or that our quest for immortality is just an ancient yearning.

The British author Malcolm Muggeridge wrote: "I had a notion that somehow, besides questing, I was being pursued." To me, it seems far more logical that there is a Divine Designer. Even more wondrous is that He wants to be a part of our lives. Occasionally, He gives us a tender shove or a gentle nudge to let us know He's nearby.

You Are Never Alone

*God has, after all, promised us nothing . . . but Himself. He does
not promise us a detour around our problems, but a guided
tour through them.*

—Anonymous

A diminutive nun mesmerized the city's politicians and lobbyists
at the 1994 National Prayer Breakfast. More than three thousand
power mongers gathered at the Hilton Hotel in Washington to hear the
"angel of Calcutta," better known as Mother Teresa.

Nothing about her attire or manner denoted strength. In fact, the
familiar blue-striped head covering reminded me of the tea towels used

in my mother's kitchen back in the forties. Even standing on a small box, her head could barely be seen above the large podium built for far more physically and politically imposing figures. The deep furrows along her cheeks and forehead, her hunched shoulders and small frame hidden beneath the white habit only reinforced her humility.

She had seemingly transcended all the things that we mortals fight each day—doubt, fear, selfishness, ambition. Several years later, after her death at the age of eighty-seven, I was stunned to learn of her troublesome doubts. How could a woman considered by many to be the world's only living saint question the goodness of God or even His existence? Yet from her own hand, we learn of her spiritual anguish. "I feel just that terrible pain of loss, of God not wanting me, of God not being God, of God not really existing," she wrote to a spiritual advisor.

We now know that Mother Teresa was a lot like the rest of us. She possessed no special holiness gene to assuage her inner feelings. Instead, she joined other frustrated religious stalwarts, suffering bouts of despair.

What Mother Teresa saw as the "hiddeness of God," Sister Teresa of Avila called the "dark night of the soul." It was what Job felt as he sat upon his ash heap mourning the loss of his family, cattle, land, and wealth. King David bemoaned his emptiness, "I sought Him . . . I look for Him on the left and on the right, but He is not there." All suffered rampant doubt—the sudden feeling of being abandoned by God, who earlier had been so apparent.

Doubting Your Doubts

Like a patch of weeds, doubt grows along the edges of faith, trying to push through any cracks that might appear. Daily—sometimes hourly—we decide whether faith or doubt will be allowed to take root in our lives.

Still, it came as a surprise when an old friend told me she was giving up on God. I had always credited her with teaching me that faith and intellect could co-exist; no need to give up one for the other, she had insisted.

But during middle age, when her dreams sputtered and her prayers went unanswered, she made an extraordinary decision. She would cease to believe! God had not produced as advertised.

It was a childlike reaction, but she was angry at the time. She stopped reading her Bible, stopped going to church, stopped teaching Sunday school as she had for years, and stopped seeing her church-going friends. She literally wiped the slate clear of her God-life . . . or so she thought.

"There was still one thing I kept on doing," she said with some puzzlement. "Instinctively and almost without realizing, I kept on praying. I could not stop, even when I tried," she later told me.

We laughed. She was trying so hard to dump God and found it very hard work. We concluded that it was not so much her holding on to God, but Him not letting go of her, even in her doubt.

I have several dear friends and relatives who tell me they don't believe in God any longer. I tell them not to worry, God still believes in them. (Like Tennyson, I "lean to the sunny side of doubt.")

I've decided that my friends have just discarded their childhood versions of God. They question a deity who sits on a cloud and hurls down thunderbolts and tsunami in his spare time. You know, the guy with the long beard, who's always peering over your shoulder, wagging a divine finger at your misdeeds. Erasing those images is actually a good first step. By doing so, they are growing closer to God than they think.

Where Is God?

Where is God when we hurt? When we are frightened? When we are alone? Is God just playing a divine version of hide-and-seek with us mortals? Or, worse yet, is He merely a celestial gadfly, flitting capriciously in and out of our lives?

We're not the first to ask. In the storm-tossed boat, the disciples awakened Jesus. "Don't you care that we are about to die?" they cried out. Jesus calmed the sea but most important, he calmed their fears.

One day I came home from work, walked in the door, and, as usual, called out for my father. But no one answered. I searched the house, called the neighbors. I couldn't find him anywhere. I was frantic. He was not in the habit of walking off. Where could he be? I broadened my search and finally found him in the garden, weeding the vegetables.

"Of course, I'm here. Where else would I be?" he asked, surprised by my doubt. That's the way God the Father reacts toward our disbelief. We must trust God even when He appears to be tending the garden elsewhere. He has not walked out of our lives. The absence we feel is temporary; it is not a permanent loss.

Faced with illness, trouble, despair, or danger, we can count on the sufficiency of grace. Author Anne Lamott describes such grace as water wings that hold us up. In one of the most emphatic of biblical promises, we are told, "I will never, no, never, leave thee, nor ever forsake thee."

He is always where we are—which is both a scary and soothing thought.

What to Do in the Meanwhile

Believers suffering from a bout of "separation anxiety" are told to wait patiently upon the Lord. But George MacDonald, the nineteenth-century writer who was such a great influence on C. S. Lewis, suggested something more. His advice was to work and wait.

"Think of something you ought to do and go do it," he writes. "Sweep the room, prepare a meal, visit a friend . . . don't heed your feelings, do your work."

St. Paul offered similar counsel: Put fear and worry behind you and reach out for what's ahead. "Press on," he declared in his letter to the Romans. (Katharine Hepburn's advice was "Plow on," but you get the idea.) Don't fret over your feelings. Trust what you know to be true, not what you feel to be true.

When I lived in the city, a trip to my next-door neighbor's house was only a few steps across the yard. After moving to the country, it was an uphill hike through the woods to see my closest neighbor.

I learned to take a flashlight with me in the event it was dark when I returned home. I remember a few nights when it was pitch black, not a star in the sky. With my small light I would start in the direction of my house, knowing it was somewhere in the darkness. The beam cast just enough light for me to see a short distance ahead, so I didn't bump into a tree.

Using the light I had and moving slowly along the path, I would arrive safely at home. Faith is taking the next step with just the small amount of light we have, confident that there is a path and that we can find it even in the gloomiest night.

The Great Certainty

One of the stories that inspired this chapter comes from a woman searching for a spiritual recovery following the loss of her five-year-old child in an automobile accident. When I first read of the incident, nearly thirty years ago, I could not relate to the deep sorrow that the mother felt. My own life was carefree and rosy, my four children hearty and healthy.

The story of this grieving mother remained in my heart over the years. I recalled it as I wallowed in the swamp of self-pity that swept over me after the loss of my husband and son and, eleven months later, the loss of my home by fire. I know now that what I felt is not unusual. I was passing through "the dark night of the soul," when God seems unreachable and nothing makes sense.

Such was the case with the mother in this story. She was searching for answers, desperately trying to move through her bereavement. She had a friend, a flight attendant, who frequently flew the route to India.

The distraught mother pleaded with her friend to find a way to talk with Mother Teresa on her behalf.

"I know that Mother Teresa will understand my hurt. She will have a message for me, if only you can get an appointment to see her."

The friend knew that it would be difficult, but she persisted and was finally granted a meeting with the revered nun. Mother Teresa listened quietly to the young woman as she recounted the heartrending incident. As the visit was about to conclude, the flight attendant asked for some words of hope to take back home to her friend.

Mother Teresa reached out, taking the hand of the young woman into her own. Looking into her outstretched palm, she said softly, "The answer is right here . . . in your hand."

"What do you mean?" the attendant asked.

"Take your friend the message of these five words," she said. Then, pointing to each finger as she spoke, she said, "I . . . am . . . with . . . you . . . ALWAYS.

"This is God's promise to your friend. She must recall it each time she looks into her hand. If she acts on that promise, she will recover."

And with that, she folded the young lady's hand tightly in hers, as if to seal the promise. The article from which I read this story ended by stating that the message was received with a grateful and believing heart. Time alone would judge the efficacy of the treatment.

But I have no doubt that it worked. It has for so many. It has for me.

His Presence is what I call the Great Certainty—the assurance that we are never beyond God's love and care. This wondrous truth has been passed down through the ages from one aching, yearning, questioning heart to another.

"God . . . is . . . with . . . you . . . always!"

That ancient promise brightened the life of a twelve-year-old Jewish girl hiding from the Nazis in a dark, third-floor attic during World War II. Ann Frank wrote, "I know the sun is shining even when I cannot see it. I know that God is living even when He does not show Himself." She held a bold and defiant hope despite everything she felt and saw to the contrary.

Albert Camus revealed his inner certainty when he wrote, "In the midst of winter, I discovered there was within me an invincible summer." God's presence warms our bleakest days and brightens the darkest nights. He is there in good times and bad, in heartache and joy, in sadness and in gladness.

We are not alone.

The Whole World in His Hands

As a teenager, I occasionally went on a weekend retreat with my church youth group. Once when I returned home, my mother asked what I had learned from the speakers.

I drew a blank. I had a boyfriend at the time, so my attention had been somewhat diverted. Finally, I remembered one speaker who had mentioned a verse that caught my attention.

I said, "I learned that God wears a tattoo."

"What did you say?" she responded in a tone of disbelief.

"God wears a tattoo. It's in the Bible."

Remember, this was the late 1940s, when tattoos were most often worn by sailors and convicts. My mother was irate.

She said, "I didn't spend eight dollars (things were a lot cheaper then) for you to come back with that kind of nonsense."

I had already developed the habit of underlining anything I read that I wanted to remember, so I turned quickly to Isaiah 49:16.

"Look, it says so right here: 'I will not forget you. See, I have inscribed you on the palm of my hands.' What about that? God has a tattoo with everybody's name on it," I said.

"Well," she harrumphed. "There must be better verses than that for you to spend your time learning."

Despite my mother's disapproval of a tattooed deity, the image is a powerful reminder that we are ever in His presence.

Alone in the Dark

The first time the electric power went out at my farm house, I was all alone. I stumbled through the darkness until I found a candle. From its faint flicker, I was able to dial the rural electric company to report the outage.

The woman who answered the phone was comforting.

"Don't worry," she said soothingly, "we know all about it. There are workers on the scene making the repairs. Everything will be all right very soon."

When I hung up the phone, I was still in the dark, but I felt a whole lot better. Someone knew about my problem and was taking care of it, so I went to bed. When I awoke, sure enough, the power had been restored.

God is not like the parents of Hansel and Gretel; He does not leave us to stumble around in the darkness alone. Whether we know it or not, He is behind the scenes working on our problems and seeking to restore our lives. In the darkest hours of our lives, His promises are ours: "Don't be afraid. I've got your hand. We're in this together."

Finding Our Core

Whether we're sitting angrily in stalled traffic or waiting anxiously at the bedside of a deathly ill loved one, we all yearn for a source of calm and certitude. We search for a known point much as the early seafarers scanned the heavens for the North Star, knowing it was immovable and dependable.

Establishing this point of certainty gives life its core. Once it is fixed, we can accomplish the extraordinary and endure the unimaginable. Without it, we are condemned to muddle through life without a point of reference. Our core of certitude houses the values and beliefs that we want to hold on to for later use. All that we have found to be true and valuable, is lodged there ready to guide us.

St. Paul proclaimed his amazing certitude when he wrote that nothing could separate us from the love of God—not death or life, not angels or powers, or things present or things to come, not height or depth, nor any creature.

God has promised us nothing but Himself. His Presence is the Great Certainty. Though at times He is demanding, his guidance is steadfast and assuring. We grow to love Him and depend on Him. And, in time, become more like Him.

Patience Pays Off

Patience is the ability to idle your motor when you feel like stripping your gears.

—Barbara Johnson, author

I've tried every fad diet, crash diet, and guaranteed-to-shed-pounds gimmick that's come along. That's why I was suspicious when some years ago a friend told me she had dropped twenty pounds on a plan of her own design. It was not a diet, she said. It was a "mindset" for "diminished calorie intake."

"It's simple." she said excitedly. "You don't have to count calories. You just set your mind instead. That's where it has to begin."

"Tell me more," I said, sucker that I am for anything that sounds easy and quick.

"Okay," she said. "Let's start by standing in front of this full-length mirror."

I approached the mirror with some caution, the way we always do after a certain number of years and pounds.

"Now, ask yourself, 'Is this the me I want to be?'"

I looked at the pudgy figure in the mirror and mentally repeated the question.

"Assuming your answer is no," my mindreading friend concluded, "now ask: 'Who do I want to be?'"

I was cautious in responding. This was already becoming too much of a brain game.

"Well . . . I want to be a person who is healthy," I said as if there was some right or wrong answer upon which I was being graded.

"That's good," she said. "What else?"

"Uhh . . . energetic."

"Keep going," she said.

"Confident . . . "

I was on a roll now!

"I want to be able to walk up hills! To ride a bicycle comfortably! To run with my grandchildren! To get into last year's green suit! I want a cinnamon roll for breakfast . . . Whoops! How did that sneak in there?"

"Okay, that's a good stopping point," she replied. "Let's examine that last wish. Picture yourself eating that cinnamon roll smothered in sugary icing and oozing melted butter that runs down your arm and drips off your elbow."

"Yes, yes!" I said teasingly.

"Now, picture eating a second roll and nibbling the edges of a third. Picture yourself devouring the whole pan of rolls with gusto."

Never had I done such a thing. But in my mind I forced myself to indulge.

"How did that make you feel?" she asked.

"It was disgusting."

"That's the point. Look at everything you eat in the extreme and it will seem less enticing."

"Okay," I said, "I'll give it a try."

That afternoon I had a lunch appointment and decided to test out the new mindset that my friend had guaranteed would diminish my calorie intake.

I pondered the menu. Would it be the half-pound mushroom burger with fries or the yogurt chicken salad on pita bread?

I pictured the burger dripping with grease on a cold, soggy bun. The fries limp, slimy, and falling from the side of the plate.

I clicked off the picture. That's enough. That decision was made. But there was another yet to come.

"Dessert, anyone?" beamed the 105-pound waitress. Buttressed with success, I was strong enough now to play her game.

"Tempt me," I said. "What do you have?"

As she described each dessert, I saw the cheesecake become a sticky paste that clung to the roof of my mouth.

The Black Forest cake became a platter of syrupy crumbs topped with a mountain of whipped cream that oozed all over my face, hair, and ears as I tried to eat it.

But the mango sorbet! That sounded refreshing. Cool. Exotic.

I saw myself in a hammock stretched between two palm trees being served fresh mango slices by native dancers. I quickly ordered the sorbet, before the illusion faded.

Thanks to my friend's advice, I still go on this non-diet occasionally. I don't lose all that much weight, but it makes me conscious of what I'm ordering or cooking. Like any game, or diet, it takes patience and practice. As my friend reminded me: victory, sweet victory is the ultimate "dessert."

We all know that impatience can cause stress, irritate the digestive system, raise blood pressure, and harm the heart, as well as personal relationships. But medical study now associates overweight with an unwillingness to forgo present satisfaction for future benefits. At least, we no longer have to blame weight gain wholly on faulty metabolism. There is another culprit: impatience.

Impatience Easily Learned

One of my earliest lessons in impatience came as a youngster waiting for a city bus, watching my fellow passengers fume and fidget nervously.

Some would peer at their watches, pace the pavement, or punch the air. When an over-loaded bus passed us by, I knew that my vocabulary of four-letter words was about to increase.

I concluded that adults had more pressing engagements than I did, giving them more cause for anxiety about a late bus. I was merely going to a weekly piano lesson that I was glad to cut short. My impatience was directed toward such things as the long waits between birthdays, Christmas, and school vacations.

I developed more impatience with age, including one habit that annoys me to this day: a compulsion to flip through a magazine from the back to the front or to sneak a peek at the last chapter of a book.

A friend once gave me a recipe for twenty-one-day pickles, with a note at the bottom that read, "With patience comes pickles." I tried the recipe once, before reverting to Heinz, which requires absolutely no patience and is nearly as good. I have struggled to moderate my eagerness to complete a task quickly. Fortunately, I married a man of infinite fortitude and learned to be less ruffled.

If patience is a prolonged effort toward a future goal, as it is sometimes described, then my husband's political career was an ideal example. He dreamed of running for public office ever since we were high school sweethearts. His education, his interests, his hopes all focused on that one goal.

He got off to a quick start when he was elected municipal judge at age twenty-five, then moved on to be state legislator the next year, and became majority floor leader of the Missouri House by age twenty-eight.

But when he ran for the state senate in the sixties, he slammed into a political brick wall. With his political career severed by defeat, he returned to practicing law, hoping another opportunity would come.

He waited . . . and waited. Five years passed. Ten years . . . nothing. It would be fourteen years before he had another chance. In 1979 he ran for state treasurer and this time he won.

During those fourteen years, when it seemed like his dreams had evaporated, I never heard him fret. Although it seemed like a prolonged hibernation, he engaged in a number of worthwhile pursuits.

While presiding over the local school board, he got a bond issue passed for a new middle school in our community. He headed the building committee to erect a new sanctuary for our church, became active in a civic club, and worked to help others seeking public office. We raised four children and found a place in the country we would all enjoy.

Waiting is not passive; it is growing, forceful, and transforming. It is more than a weary interlude. The interval of waiting is a formative time during which God shapes our lives more in His likeness.

The "Microwave Generation"

We live in a society of the impatient, the eager, and the rarin' to go. We have been called the "microwave generation," because we want everything ASAP. (Even those words are condensed to an acronym to make them fly off our tongue faster.)

Our financial system encourages instant gratification, with credit card lenders eager to accommodate our yearnings. Businesses appeal to their fast-moving customers by offering swift services. Not only are we attracted to fast food and instant messaging, but Jiffy Lube, QwikPrint, 1-hour photo, and One-Stop Shopping. We get out of sorts with computers, cell phones, and iPods that fail to perform as promised. Appliance makers have learned to print instruction booklets in abbreviated form for consumers who refuse to read the manual.

We are distraught when the weather doesn't cooperate with our plans, the phone rings one too many time, or healing takes longer than we anticipated. Agitation sets in when we dash into the grocery store for one item and discover the fellow in the ten-items-or-fewer lane has fifteen items, which he is meticulously counting out while apologizing to the clerk. Traffic jams and bad drivers are some of the worst irritants. The definition of a split second is the length of time between the stop light turning green and the guy behind you honking his horn.

During even a brief interval of waiting, we see things differently than if we plunged forward on our first impulse. We gather the strength and insight that come from taking a mental interlude.

Rules for the Terminally Impatient

While patience is a virtue that has eluded both saints and seers, it is not beyond our grasp. Like any other trait, it can be learned and improved over time. Though I have worked for years to develop greater patience, I admit to only modest gains. Below are my *Rules for the Terminally Impatient*.

> **Be patient with yourself.** Take one day at a time. Don't try to become patient all at once. (A true sign of impatience.) Pick one aspect of your life that's bothersome, perhaps your frustration with a coworker or with motorists on the highway. Building patience is much like building muscle strength. It takes regular and painful practice to see results.
>
> **Set your watch ahead.** This really works. It gives you a cushion. As little as ten minutes of extra time can greatly reduce your aggravation and lessen the likelihood of your being late for an appointment, driving too fast, or leaving something important undone. If morning is your bad time, set your alarm fifteen minutes early, lay out your clothes the night before, and place everything you want to take with you near the door.
>
> **Admit your impatience.** Use the Ronald Reagan line. Say to yourself, "There you go again, being impatient." Identify what triggers your response. Treat your impatience like a trespasser and take immediate steps to oust the intruder from the premises of your mind.

Try planned persistence. Many years ago I learned a mental trick from a salesman. He told me that in order to rack up one sale, he had to make seven calls, on the average. "I have learned to make rejection part of my success," he said. "You have to get through the layers of refusals to find the purchaser waiting to be discovered." Later, as a political candidate, I adopted my friend's plan and raised millions of campaign dollars on the telephone. Along the way, I collected plenty of rejections and excuses, but I treated them as a necessary part of reaching my goal.

Find the humor. Think what a funny story you will have to tell at the dinner table or on your coffee break. When you can turn an ordeal into a hee-haw, you've uncovered one of the greatest of stress relievers.

Look for the lesson. Ask if there is anything good to be learned from the experience. That is what I asked myself one day after misplacing my keys and getting locked out of my car. After *five* friendly advisors . . . *four* phone calls . . . *three* hours of wait . . . *two* surly locksmiths . . . and *one* humongous bill, I gained entry. Now I have a hide-a-key magnet box that can be slipped into some exterior crevice of the car. I have forgotten or misplaced my keys several times since then, but I now smile smugly as I pull out the hidden key and drive away.

Plant a garden. The Japanese say the way to gain patience is to sit and watch the rocks grow—though gardening is far more productive. Planting seeds and waiting for growth puts us in sync with nature and reminds us that the universe is not set to our watch. If you stick with it, you will grow both plants and patience.

Grow old. Aging is the ultimate teacher of patience. Coping with the indignities of growing old requires as many virtues as we can muster, but patience is the most important. As we spend more time searching for eyeglasses, fiddling with pills and hearing aids, struggling up stairs, and taking longer to do just about everything, we eventually learn the patience that eluded us during our youth.

Take command. Yes, there are annoying people in the world, frustrating situations, unexplained delays, and setbacks that can trigger an angry response—if we allow it. These unwanted circumstances and people must not shape who we are or how we will react at any given moment. We are not puppets on a string controlled by others. We decide how we will react.

Freedom

A nation is never finished. You cannot build it and then leave it standing as the Pharaohs did the pyramids. It has to be recreated for each generation by believing, caring men and women. It is now our turn. If we don't care, nothing can save the nation. If we believe and care, nothing can stop us.

—John Gardner, author and educator

Freedom Is Never Free

*What is the use of living if it be not to strive for noble causes and
to make this muddled world a better place for those who will
have it after we are gone?*

—Winston Churchill

I was only eight years old. My parents and I were enjoying a Sunday afternoon drive along the Tidal Basin in Washington, D.C., when the announcer on the car radio interrupted the Sunday afternoon broadcast to inform us that the Japanese had bombed Pearl Harbor.

I had no idea what that meant. But I remember well my parent's reactions: the stunned look on my father's face, the anxious tone in my mother's voice. I had never before seen my parents frightened. This was serious.

But, who were the Japanese?

Where was Pearl Harbor?

What did this mean to us?

During those uncertain days following the attack, my parents and all Americans turned to the man who had led the nation out of the Great Depression: President Franklin D. Roosevelt. He spoke of "inevitable triumph" at a time when we had an Army smaller than the Swedes, the Congress was debating the size of our cavalry, and half our navy lay at the bottom of the sea.

In what would become known as FDR's fireside chats, he summoned a bewildered nation to the formidable task of waging a world war. As it turned out, the Japanese had aroused a sleeping giant. Roosevelt called for the building of 50,000 planes a year, ten times the current output. He challenged American industry to build a ship a day, and they did. He asked for a stern commitment, not only from industry, but from civilians and military alike. At first, such a grand mobilization seemed impossible, but the idea captured the imagination of the American people.

We understood the battle was for the survival of democracy. There was no outsourcing of this fight.

It was ours.

A line from one of the wartime songs reflected our common resolve: "Buckle down, Buck Private, buckle down. We can win this war, if we only buckle down." And buckle down we did.

As we geared up for war, Americans accepted the inconveniences and made the necessary adjustments to support the effort. President Roosevelt described the mobilization as "One front and one battle where everyone in the United States—every man, woman, and child—is in action."

In my family that meant my mother giving up her job as a hairdresser and going to work for the Navy Department as a file clerk. Daddy, too old for the draft, took on several jobs in addition to serving as a volunteer air raid warden for our block. During the practice drills, he would strap on his white helmet and patrol the streets, armed only with the nightstick that was standard civilian defense attire. His mission was to see that everyone remained indoors with lights extinguished and blackout shades secured. In the days before precision bombing, a darkened city made it more difficult for the enemy to see its targets.

Daddy and I clipped pictures and articles from the newspaper and put together a scrapbook tracing the advance of our army across Europe and the Pacific islands. As the war progressed, my father walked me through every military display of tanks, submarines, warships, and aircraft that was put on exhibit to keep Americans in touch with their war.

Our family also looked out for our next-door neighbor, whose husband was serving in Europe. In her front window hung a small banner with a blue star, indicating that a member of the household was on active duty. Loved ones killed during the war were commemorated with a Gold Star banner, and Gold Star Mothers formed as a support group for those who had lost a son in battle.

Wartime also brought shortages and rationing that limited sugar, coffee, meat, butter, cheese, tires, and gasoline. Daddy planted a victory garden that kept our family and neighbors supplied with fresh vegetables each summer. "Can all you can" was the wartime slogan, and we did. Mama lined our basement shelves with jars of tomatoes, green beans, beets, sauerkraut, pickles, and chowchow—enough to see us through another Thirty Years War.

Meatless Tuesdays became a regular part of our wartime menus. We made do with three gallons of gas per week, unless Daddy was able to trade some sugar stamps for fuel stamps. When we did travel, we did so at the victory speed of 35 mph to save fuel. Those with an "A" gasoline sticker on their car were allowed three to four gallons of gas a week;

those in more essential jobs got a "B" or "C" sticker and more fuel, while a "T" sticker for trucks rated still more gallons.

Butter was replaced with the new oleomargarine that, at the time, looked and tasted much like lard. For those who found it disgusting to spread on toast, the ugly lump came with a packet of yellow coloring to improve its appearance.

Mostly, I missed sleeping on real cotton sheets. In a fervor of patriotism, my mother made sheets from feed sacks. It was her answer to the material shortage. Six bags, split along the sides, bleached to remove the printing, and sewn together produced a sturdy but scratchy bed covering. There were even special patterns for making aprons, shirts, and dresses from feed sacks. When I fussed about such austerity, Mama let me know that it was a small sacrifice to make, knowing that our soldiers were sleeping in foxholes and on cots. Like others who complained about wartime shortages and hardships, I was cut short with the reminder, "We're at war, don't you know?"

One of the happy occasions following the end of the war was seeing Mama pull out the old percale sheets she had stowed away for The Duration. Those indestructible feed sacks survived the war and went on for decades to serve as camping gear, drop cloths, and dust rags. During the era of make-do and re-do, wartime families learned the virtues of recycling long before it was an environmental virtue.

The Children's War

Kids did their part on the home front, too. I collected old newspapers that I sold to the scrap yard for 50 cents per hundred pounds; magazines fetched 75 cents. My sales provided me with ample money for comic books and enough to invest in some $18.87 war bonds that held the promise of a $25 repayment a decade later.

Living in the nation's capital meant we were the target of a potential bombing attack, and we rehearsed for such an event. At my grade school, students were fingerprinted for identification purposes as we prepared for the possibility of an air attack. When a warning siren shrieked an alert during school hours, students headed for the hallway and crouched against the wall with heads down until the all-clear siren sounded.

School children also learned to identify planes in the sky from their silhouettes, so we would be able to report any suspicious aircraft sighting. We felt safe at night knowing that huge searchlights from nearby airbases scanned the skies for any sign of enemy aircraft.

Of course, the nation's capital was never bombed, but each Saturday at the theater we saw newsreels of air battles and bombings on the other side of the world. Our parents and teachers soothed our fears by reminding us that we were "an ocean away" from any battlefield and thus insulated from such horrors.

Not only did the war affect our school day, it also gave us a new vocabulary of words and phrases: *ration book, 4-F, 1-A, GIs, draft dodger, jeep, gremlins, USO, Blitzkrieg, Gestapo, Quisling, goose stepping, kamikaze, U-boat, Axis,* and *Luftwaffe.*

My most creative defense project was organizing the kids into an army prepared to defend the neighborhood in the event the Japanese should reach the shores of the Anacostia River and march on S Street. Like the patriots of old, we each brought our own arms, which in our case consisted of toy rifles or wood poles. I supplied them with insignias from my prized collection in hopes of instilling some military spirit in the ranks. They were a frustrating bunch to command, inept at following orders, marching in step, or even showing up on time.

I finally decided I would have to go it alone. If the war would last just seven more years, I could join the women's Marine Corps. In the meanwhile, I would go back to collecting scrap paper and expanding my insignia collection.

I never got over the patriotism that we felt during those years of uncertainty and sacrifice. We were at our best as a people, confident of our national purpose.

"Nothing Like Us Ever Was"

Patriotism was fired by films such as *Mrs. Miniver*, a Greer Garson and Walter Pidgeon favorite that showed the hardships of a middle-class English family during the Blitz. The film, which Churchill said was more powerful than "a hundred battleships," won six Oscars in 1942 and went a long way toward breaking down the isolationist temperament in America.

In the spirit of the times, we baked cookies to fill CARE packages and rolled bandages with the Red Cross. We wrote letters to friends and relatives abroad, using a tissue-thin paper that folded into an envelope and required a special APO address. Several of my teenage cousins joined the military. I kept up a lively correspondence with one stationed in Germany; the other was killed before I got his overseas address.

We tracked the D-Day invasion as our troops dug in along the Normandy beachhead and advanced village by village across Europe. We followed the battles of Generals Patton, Eisenhower, MacArthur, and Bradley, as well as Admiral Nimitz. From film clips shown in movie theaters, we saw the hideous scenes of Nazi concentration camps and the Bataan Death March.

Before the day of television, these short films gave us a glimpse of the Allies in action, bombing cities and engaging in gun battles at sea, in the air, and on the ground. I shared the sadness that we all felt learning of the casualties and hardships endured by both soldiers and civilians.

It was a high point in our slog across France when our soldiers reached Paris—at least it was a city we had heard of. With the pomp of the Roman legions returning from the Gallic wars, our troops marched beneath the Arc de Triomphe receiving the accolades reserved for conquering heroes.

By 1945, victory in Okinawa gave our military the needed stepping stone for a land invasion of Japan. But the grim battle showed that an attack on the Japanese homeland would be a long and costly assault. With the atomic bombing of Hiroshima and Nagasaki, the Japanese forces saw the futility of the fight and surrendered.

America and her allies had taken on brutal and overpowering foes and prevailed. Like the patriots of old, we were infused with high resolve and uncommon courage. Carl Sandburg was right when he said, "We are Americans; nothing like us ever was."

A Noble Cause

So what does a child take away from such an unnatural time?

During those formative years, I witnessed two great world leaders join hand and heart to change the course of history. Franklin Roosevelt and Winston Churchill inspired us to be our best, to defy every obstacle, and to meet every challenge.

During the worst bombings of London, Churchill had told the school boys of Harrow, "Do not let us speak of darker days; let us speak rather of sterner days. These are not dark days; these are great days—the greatest days our country has ever lived . . . "

What a contrast to 9/11, when Americans, waiting to be called to action, were told to go shopping at the mall. Our military—the best in the world—would take care of things quickly and be home for supper—a feat that B-2 bomber pilots were literally able to do. Our response to world terrorism required something more of us, but we were never asked.

The opportunity to seize the 9/11 moment to create a new energy policy for the 21st century was also lost. A call for less dependency on foreign oil could have transformed our society. Sadly, the chance for creating national unity and grand purpose was squandered.

There was no Roosevelt or Churchill to rally us to "lofty enthusiasm" or to urge "a toughness of moral and physical fiber"; no film like *Mrs. Miniver* in which we were told: "This is not only a war of soldiers in uniform; it is a war of the people—of all the people."

Those of my generation understood the need for noble causes lead by stalwart leaders. We knew that national purpose could not be achieved on the cheap, without direction, or alone.

Fortunately, in a democracy there are chances to start anew.

One Person Can Make a Difference

If you stand for a reason, be prepared to stand alone like a tree.
If you fall to the ground, fall as a seed that
grows back to fight again.

—Anonymous

"Why are you a Democrat?" I sometimes ask people who seem particularly passionate about politics. "What event, or person, nudged you in that direction?" What I hear is not an academic explanation, comparing political parties or candidates. Most often I am told a heartwarming story.

There was a time when we were defined by a narrative that every Democrat family could tell—stories of hardship, injustice, or hopelessness. We connected with the Democratic Party, which sought to alleviate those wrongs with fair labor laws, civil rights legislation, and social and educational programs for working men and women.

One such story came from a man in his eighties who visited my Senate office. His name is Bernard Rappaport, and he is one of the wealthiest men in Texas. He goes by his first initial, B. I asked B why he was a Democrat—why, at his age, he bothered to walk the halls of the Capitol pushing for health care and worker benefits. He told me that his father was a Jewish immigrant who sold blankets from a pushcart on the streets of Waco.

One day B was hit by a car that badly injured his leg. The family couldn't afford any more than routine medical care, so his leg just healed in nature's way. As he pointed to the sizeable lift on the heel of one shoe, he said, "Each morning when I put on my shoes, I'm reminded of the health care needs of children."

His story shaped who he was, what he believed, and what he was willing to fight for all his life.

My Story

I recently met an immigrant from a small African village who was working and going to school in Montana. He contrasted the hopelessness he felt in his native land with the opportunities he now has as an American citizen.

"In America, anything is possible," he said with great enthusiasm. He is right. His children will be the beneficiaries of public education, student and business loans, and possibly even health care. In *one generation*, his family will likely make a gigantic leap forward, one that is undreamed of in most cultures.

What a contrast to my family of Scotch-Irish and German settlers, which arrived in rural Virginia early in the 18th century. Generation after generation, they eked out a hardscrabble living on small farms, with little hope of life ever being any better. No matter how hard they worked, it seemed they would always be a part of the underclass.

But thanks to the Democratic Party, all that changed in one generation—*my generation!* Three hundred years after my ancestors set foot on these shores, I became the first in my family to graduate from both high school and college.

Here's my story:

When I was five, my parents bought their first home. The subdivision, located in southeast Washington, was built as America was coming out of the Depression and people were trying to get back on their feet.

On a vacant lot across the street was a large billboard that read, NEW FHA HOMES FOR SALE, $5,590. NO MONEY DOWN. GOVERNMENT-INSURED LOAN. Roosevelt's new recovery program was responsible for financing the several hundred semi-detached homes built in sets of three, all looking alike.

I was young, but I can still remember how proud my parents were of our new home. They had never before owned a house of their own. My grandparents had never owned a home. For us, this was the American dream.

Every time we bought a piece of new furniture for our home, every time we planted a new rose bush in the backyard or took in a relative who had fallen on hard times, we knew we had been given a golden opportunity—the chance for home ownership.

Social Security and Medicare also gave families like ours hope for the future. My grandfather, a union carpenter, benefited from the 40-hour week and minimum-wage legislation. When he died, leaving my grandmother a widow for the next twenty years without savings or income, Social Security was there for her, put into place by FDR and a Democratic Congress.

My husband's family had a story, as well. His father, the first of the Carnahans to graduate from college, became a teacher and eventually a school superintendent in what was one of the poorest areas in Missouri. Using government commodities, my father-in-law created the first hot lunch program in the Ozarks to ensure that students got at least one nutritious meal a day.

As a youngster, my husband lived in a farm house newly lighted by the Rural Electrification Administration (REA), established by Roosevelt because private companies thought it was too expensive to serve isolated areas.

He attended law school on the GI Bill following the Korean War. Our children graduated from public high schools and attended college on student loans. Title 9 legislation meant that my daughter had the opportunity to play team sports in high school. During the same era, the enormous gains in civil rights, women's rights, and human rights would bring further opportunities to disadvantaged Americans.

Garrison Keillor was right: "Milk comes from cows and Medicare comes from Democrats." Opportunity comes from Democrats, too. I don't have to defend that to anyone. I saw it happen.

An Infamous Day

As these stories show, Democrats have a history of improving people's lives, protecting rights, and providing opportunity. Standing up for the powerless is an underlying theme of the Democratic Party.

One horrendous event that triggered reform in the workplace occurred in 1911. The tragedy that stirred the soul of the nation would be the catalyst for improving the shameful conditions in factories employing young women and children in America.

The Triangle Shirtwaist Factory, located on the ninth floor of a downtown building in New York City, employed immigrant girls between the ages of thirteen and twenty-three. The unsanitary and dangerous working conditions were typical of sweatshops during the era. The young women sat behind their sewing machines for long hours, earning $9 for a fifty-six-hour week. Instead of getting overtime for working additional hours, they were given a slice of apple pie.

A sign at the top of the rickety wooden steps leading to the workroom read: IF YOU DON'T COME IN ON SUNDAY, DON'T COME IN ON MONDAY.

It was the practice of the management to keep the doors locked, so no one could leave without permission. Near closing time on March 25, 1911, a fire broke out. The doors, as usual, were locked. The horse-drawn fire trucks answered the call, but the ladders were too short to reach the upper floor; the hoses were not long enough to reach the fire; and the nets broke when the women jumped.

In fifteen minutes' time, 146 women perished in what was the worst fire in New York history. Several years later, after much litigation, twenty-three of the families were each awarded $75 for the loss of their loved ones.

Sitting in a nearby restaurant that day having tea with friends, listening to the fire bells sound the alarm, was a woman named Frances Perkins. She stood on the street and watched helplessly a scene she would never forget. The tragedy became part of her story, one that would drive her to organize groups of inspectors to march through old factories, insisting that changes be made. When Roosevelt went to Washington, he called on Frances Perkins to be his Secretary of Labor— the first woman to ever hold a cabinet position.

Before accepting his offer, she told the president, "Don't call me to Washington, unless you mean to turn me loose." And he agreed. She arrived with a handwritten list of demands for minimum wages, safe working conditions, unemployment compensation, and Social Security. Ultimately, these programs became the core of the New Deal.

Democrats Today

Justice and opportunity are always at risk. We must continue the fight because there are still kids like B. Rappaport who are not getting the medical treatment they need. There are still people who yearn for their own home in a safe neighborhood, with affordable child care and successful schools, as I did and my parents did. There are still workers struggling in low-benefit jobs who are just one paycheck, just one illness, away from homelessness, as my grandfather was. Like Frances Perkins, we are still standing up for the voiceless and the vulnerable, the hurting and the elderly.

We can be instruments of change anytime we determine to fix a problem or right a wrong. I recall reading the story of a little black girl named Tessie, who lived in Louisiana back in the sixties. During the desegregation of the public schools, she was escorted to class each day by federal marshals. For months she walked past an angry mob, shouting obscenities and threats.

Years later a researcher looked up these students to get their recollections of that stressful time. One of those interviewed was Tessie.

"You were only six years old; where did you get the strength and courage to face such an intimidating mob each day?" she was asked.

"It was something my grandmother told me. She said, 'Child, we have to help the good Lord with his world! He puts us here and He expects us to help Him out.'"

There are many opportunities to help out. How we respond to the "least among us," defines us as a people and as a party. Democrats have always stood for the things that make a difference in people's lives.

That's just the way we are.

Questioning Is Dangerous

The people I admire most in our history are the hell-raisers and the rabble-rousers, the apple-cart upsetters and plain old mumpish eccentrics who just didn't want to be like everybody else. They are the people who made and make the Constitution of the United States a living document . . .

—Molly Ivins

One evening as I was sitting around with a group of friends talking about an upcoming election, the topic turned to what we considered unique about America.

What makes us different?

One said it was our optimism and cited some statistics to show that Americans tend to view the future as being rosier than most other people of the world.

Another mentioned our ability to solve problems. "We believe that with enough effort we can find the solution to anything," he said.

I pointed out our diversity, noting that America is not a clear broth, but more of a "hearty, robust chowder with many ingredients and spices."

One brought up our competitive nature. "We want to be first, to be winners."

"Don't forget our love of liberty, equality, and justice," another chimed in. "And we love underdogs. We enjoy a good rags-to-riches story, with someone overcoming hardship."

But the one observation that stirred the most comment was: "We are a nation of dissenters." We laughed, but we all agreed. Americans are inclined to question authority. It is inherent in our genetic makeup as a nation. In a democracy, questioning is all the more necessary. Still, it always takes some daring to speak out.

When Socrates was asked what he considered his greatest accomplishment, he responded: "I taught men to question." For his efforts, the great Athenian was accused of "corruption of the young" and "neglect of the gods." Indicted for "impiety," Socrates was forced to end his days by drinking the deadly cup of hemlock. That should have put a damper on probing minds, but it didn't. In the centuries that followed, we questioned a flat earth, the divine right of kings, slavery, the treatment of diseases and mental illness, and the inferiority of women. Those today who are hacking at the roots of ignorance and injustice find their task no less grueling and dangerous than it ever was.

The Tough Questions

One of my favorite questioners was a nineteenth-century suffragette, Elizabeth "Lizzy" Cady Stanton. As a child, she would sneak into her father's law library and read the books. She was disturbed by what she read, and for good reason. She discovered that, according to the law, a woman was the property of her husband. She could not:

> . . . buy, sell, or inherit property in her own name

> . . . divorce an abusive husband or receive custody of her children

> . . . testify in court, file a law suit, or serve on a jury

> . . . vote or hold an office in her community, church, or nation

> . . . borrow or invest money in her own name

She was not even entitled to her own wages; was limited in the jobs she could hold; and ineligible to attend some colleges or to study certain subjects.

As Lizzy read the law books, she would pencil in the changes she wanted to see made. One day her father discovered what she was doing. He told her that her efforts were futile.

"Only lawmakers, who are men—elected by men—can change the laws," he reminded her. It was a pivotal moment, Lizzy recalled, when she determined to change the laws and the conditions that caused them.

Lizzy married and had seven children, but that did not squelch her interest in changing what she called the "cruelties of the laws." She became a writer and organizer, teaming up with Lucretia Mott and Susan B. Anthony in building the case for the suffrage movement. Her statements, often witty and blistering, were always insightful. She wrote, "If God has assigned a sphere to man and one to woman, we claim the right ourselves to judge His design in reference to us. We think that a man has quite enough to do to find out his own individual calling without being taxed to find out also where every woman belongs."

While I have always admired the suffragettes who challenged the traditional thinking, I appreciate their efforts even more after seeing first-hand how risky it is to question power.

You Can't Fight in the War Room

Far above the hubbub of activity in the U. S. Capitol is a quiet, highly secure room designed for classified briefings of U. S. Senators. Electronic devices and phones are checked at the door. The austere room outlined with a U-shaped table is windowless, soundproof, and regularly swept for listening devices. No staff is permitted, and no notes can be taken.

Each time I entered this sacrosanct area, I thought of the war room scene from *Dr. Strangelove* and Peter Sellers' hilarious line during a heated scuffle: "You can't fight here," he shouts. "This is the war room!"

Well, we didn't fight. (In retrospect, we should have.) Mostly we listened. We listened to Donald Rumsfeld and a passel of generals who informed us of impending threats to national security. It was hinted that Saddam had ties to al Qaeda; that by using UAVs (unmanned aerial vehicles), he could deliver biological and chemical weapons to our doorstep; and, scariest of all, that the Iraqi dictator might be developing a nuclear bomb.

It was in the "upper room" that I first heard Rumsfeld's infamous comment on our intelligence gathering capacity—a comment that could have come directly from General Turgidson in that movie war room.

"As we know, there are known knowns. There are things we know we know. We also know there are known unknowns. That is to say, we know there are some things we do not know. But there are also unknown unknowns, the ones we don't know we don't know." (No fooling, this is an exact quote, one that he repeated often.)

Deciphering such gibberish was as impossible as believing anyone could utter it in the first place. Despite the dire and cryptic warnings, some senators had doubts about the war, especially if it meant taking unilateral action. When Senate Democratic leader Tom Daschle expressed concerns, however, he was promptly put down by Republican leader Trent Lott. The Mississippi Republican erupted, "How dare Senator Daschle criticize President Bush and our war on terrorism!" The president piled on, declaring Saddam Hussein a "grave threat to the region, world, and the United States."

Thus, dissent was shut down.

No Questions Asked

The invasion of Iraq was made synonymous with waging war on terrorism and dislodging Saddam became synonymous with a 9/11 payback. Few challenged the war with much heart. There were several days of Senate debate in which some said the powers requested by President Bush were too broad and action in Iraq premature. Senator Robert Byrd, a fifty-year veteran of Washington political battles, expressed concern over the "unchecked powers" of the executive and called the war resolution a "blank check" for White House abuse.

In the House, Democratic leader Richard Gephardt supported the war and Senate leader Tom Daschle went along, feeling it was important to speak with one voice. Still many House Democrats broke away, resulting in a vote of 296–133 in favor of war, while in the Senate 23 opposed the resolution. I was among those who voted for the resolution. For me to have done otherwise in the face of those briefings would have been unconscionable.

We know now that some of those "upper room" sessions were little more than a "story hour" for senators. The case for war, which seemed so compelling then, was largely fabricated. Sadly, the tenor of the times stifled opposition and silenced the broad debate that might otherwise have occurred.

We failed to question.

As I think back on those briefings, I wonder what Prime Minister Harold MacMillan might have thought. In his biography, he recalls the warning of his freshman college professor, who declared that the sole purpose of their education was to enable them to "detect when a man is talking rot." We were listening to "rot" and, sadly, too few recognized it as such.

Questioning not only illuminates, it liberates, which is why a totalitarian government resists informing its people. A democracy, on the other hand, cannot survive without an informed and participating citizenry ready to question conventional thinking. As Elie Wiesel reminded us, "There may be times when we are powerless to prevent injustice, but there must never be a time when we fail to protest."

Words: The Weapon of Choice

Today, the Internet has opened up a whole new world for questioning that Stanton and Socrates never envisioned. Like the starship *Enterprise*, bloggers are going where no man has gone before. This can be both exhilarating and frightening, as these adventurers carve out new territory and take on new foes. Armed with a monitor, keyboard, and a mouse, they are ever alert for political spin, pretense, a revealing statistic, or an intriguing connection between events and people.

Bloggers are every bit as provocative and persistent as the Colonial pamphleteers whose incendiary writing set the stage for rebellion. Because pamphlets were cheap and easy to distribute and their source difficult to trace, Colonial pundits could easily poke fun at the King without fear of being poked back. If you held a strong opinion in those early days of our country, you opened a print shop, as Ben Franklin did. Or, like Thomas Paine, you circulated anonymous writings, such as his *Common Sense* tract that was read widely throughout the colonies.

Like those early dissenters, bloggers use catchy pen names to conceal harsh commentary, reveal hypocrisy, or expose corruption. While some may downplay their effectiveness, one thing is for sure: Bloggers are not likely to abandon their free pulpits. They are here to stay. With millions of bloggers gearing up to engage in the greatest expression of free speech in world history, politicians face a fearless and well-informed new constituency willing to ask tough questions.

Our Founding Fathers would have found such citizen participation invigorating. They felt that robust dissent was the essence of patriotism and necessary for the survival of democracy. U. S. Senator Carl Schurz of Missouri declared, "My country, right or wrong—*if right, to be kept right; and if wrong, to be set right.*"

We cannot remain indifferent. Freedom dies when we cease to care.

We must speak truth to power. It's our duty as a free people.

Patriotism Is More Than Flag Waving

Thus may the Fourth of July, that glorious and ever memorable day, be celebrated through America, by the sons of freedom, from age to age till time shall be no more. Amen and Amen.
                    —Virginia Gazette, *July 17, 1777*

Fireworks, flags, and favorite foods. All are part of the celebration of our nation's birth. The Fourth of July is a momentous date in American history—one that the Founding Fathers said should be observed with parades, fireworks, and speeches.

Our Independence Day is a proud and happy occasion, as birthday parties should be. I especially remember a few of those celebrations.

Among the very memorable was the Fourth of July that I spent in the emergency room after a firecracker accidentally exploded in my hand. But typically, I have fond memories of family picnics shared with neighbors and often visitors from other countries.

My most meaningful Fourth of July did not occur in this country. It was in Russia. In the 1980s, I traveled for three weeks in Asia and wound up in Moscow on July Fourth. The combination of bad food, poor accommodations, and Communist attitudes was beginning to wear on all of us.

As the holiday approached, I sensed some homesickness among the weary travelers. Our small colony of Americans was saddened at being away from our homeland on this special day. It would be a quiet and cheerless evening. Or so we thought.

Our spirits began to perk up when one in the group said she had a package of small American flags that she had brought along to give to children. She offered to decorate the dinner tables with them. Another suggested that we all wear something red, white, or blue to dinner. That evening our patriotic costuming offered some humor, showing how creative we could be with a suitcase of wrinkled clothing.

Our Russian guide attempted to enliven the meal, too. She announced excitedly that we would be having *hamburgers* for dinner! Meat had been in short supply during most of the trip, so that was welcome news. As it turned out, the chewy, tasteless burgers were far from the American beef we were used to eating. Still, no one complained. We knew that our guide was doing her best to give us a sense of home as we celebrated what she called "your revolution day."

At the end of the meal, we decided that no Fourth was complete without speeches. (Funny how we try to avoid those at home.) Several gave very moving remarks, with one recounting a Fourth of July spent on the battlefield. We ended the evening by singing every patriotic song we could think of. We weren't always singing in the same key, but, hey, that happens even at home.

An American couple, hearing the song drifting into the hotel lobby was thrilled to find a group of their countrymen celebrating freedom in the heart of the Soviet Union. There was not a dry eye that night as we departed for our rooms with many declaring it was their best July Fourth ever.

You Ain't Seen Nothing Yet

When living in Washington, I often passed the National Archives, the building that President Herbert Hoover called the "temple of our history" and "an expression of the American soul." I take great consolation in knowing that the Declaration of Independence and the U. S. Constitution, our national treasures passed down from our

Founding Fathers, are securely protected behind those massive bronze doors.

One of the inscriptions, from Shakespeare, is carved on the statuary surrounding the Archives. It reads: "What is past is prologue," which I like to think means, "You ain't seen nothing yet." The other, "Eternal vigilance is the price of liberty," is a good reminder that these hallowed proclamations must be kept alive by each generation.

America's founding documents have not always been housed in the National Archives. During World War II, they were taken from the Library of Congress and stored underground at Fort Knox, along with a copy of the Magna Carta. In the fifties, the documents came to reside at the National Archives, where they are now in hermetically sealed encasements filled with helium gas.

I still go to the National Archives from time to time and stand in line with the tourists. I go to remind myself that these sacred documents still exist: like myself, a few years older, but still enduring.

More recently, I climbed the long steps leading to the entrance of the National Archives and stood in line along with my eleven-year-old granddaughter. I had insisted that she take time out from viewing the relics in the nearby Museum of National History to see something that I loved.

As we approached the Declaration of Independence and the U. S. Constitution, I noticed that the noisy tourists grew respectfully silent. They seemed to sense a sacred quality about these old writings. We also took some time to view a copy of the Magna Carta that was on loan from the British. I explained to my granddaughter that the feudal document—the original dating from 1215—was designed to protect the barons of England from the abuses of the king. The idea that the king (or ruler) is bound by the law would eventually become an accepted part of English law and the foundation of our constitutional law today.

I noted that the enduring legacy of the Great Charter was the writ of *habeas corpus,* which prevents unlawful imprisonment. I explained it like this. Referring to the recent film *The Dukes of Hazzard,* I said, "What if J. D. Hogg got riled up one day and decided to toss Luke and Bo Duke behind bars and throw away the key? Could he do it?"

"I guess so," she said with some uncertainty.

"Well, the Hazzard political boss might giggle with glee at the thought, but he just couldn't do it," I explained, "thanks to a provision in our Constitution called *habeas corpus.* It essentially means: Let the person go free or else give him a trial—you many not hold him forever without charging him with a crime. Boss Hogg would then have to prove his case against the Dukes or turn them loose."

All this might have been a little much at her age, but I will explain it again the next time we visit the Archives. I hope she will learn to love these old documents as I do and come to realize that in every generation, "Eternal vigilance is the price of liberty."

What's Special About September 17?

I made a point of visiting the Archives when I was in the U. S. Senate. I already had the pocket-size copy of the documents that Senator Robert Byrd gives to each new member. The West Virginia lawmaker carries a copy of the U. S. Constitution in his vest pocket at all times. As he gave me the booklet, he reminded me that it was our duty to defend the Constitution even against those "rascals at the other end of the Avenue"—an obvious reference to those in the White House that he felt were usurping the powers of Congress.

Later I would see Byrd in action. Standing on the floor of the Senate in a pose reminiscent of Daniel Webster, he would fish the booklet from his vest pocket and with a trembling hand—but an unwavering voice—brandish the U. S. Constitution like a patriot heralding the cause of liberty.

So I was not surprised a few years later to read an article in the *Washington Post* telling of Byrd's latest attempt at making the precepts of the U. S. Constitution more widely known and appreciated. Byrd tucked an unexpected nugget deep into an appropriations bill that went unnoticed by many. The new law requires that all executive branch employees of the federal government receive "educational and training" materials about the U. S. Constitution on September 17 each year, traditionally know as Constitution Day but seldom observed.

In addition to the federal employees covered by the law, every school receiving federal funds, from grade schools to universities, is subject to the mandate. Byrd is unmoved by those who find the directive burdensome. Standing with the help of two canes, he argued forcefully that citizens must "know the fundamental principles on which their government is founded. Our Constitution is not a mere dry piece of dead parchment," the ninety-year-old statesmen argued, "but a revered and living document that has helped inspire our nation to achieve seemingly impossible goals and to keep alive irrepressible hope."

Having read the account of his newest effort to keep the Constitution alive, I searched my shelves for the booklet that Byrd had signed for me when I first went to the Senate. As he suggested, I had read the old document, underlined portions of it, and even carried it in my purse for a while, until space constraints forced it onto a nearby bookshelf.

Somehow, it didn't seem right to put it back on the bookshelf again. So I gave it to my son, Russ, who now serves in the U. S. House of

Representatives. I will not insist that he "wear it," as does Robert Byrd. But in times like these, it might be good to keep it in his desk drawer.

The Razor Edge of Danger

Most Americans have some strong feelings about what it means to live in a nation that honors liberty, justice, and equality. In 2005, when I started the online newspaper, FiredUpMissouri.com, I posted a quote from Thornton Wilder that has run each day at the top of the Web page as a reminder of my intent.

"Every good and worthwhile thing stands moment by moment on the razor edge of danger and must be fought for, whether it's a house, or a field, or a country."

In less prosaic form, I also posted my beliefs.

Life, Liberty, and the Pursuit of Happiness

I believe:

... that next to love, a good education is the best gift we can provide our children

... that government is not "them," but "us"

... that the Greatest Generation deserves more than recognition on special holidays, but the daily honor of a secure and caring society

. . . that politics is not about power, and perks, and privilege—but about improving people's lives

. . . that Social Security is not just another investment scheme, but a solemn promise

. . . that the Good Book says that how we treat the poor, the hurting, and the helpless is a measure of how we treat Him

. . . that values are better expressed by our works than by our words

. . . that one person really can make a difference and that lots of people working together can make a lot of difference

. . . and I believe that freedom is never free; it always costs somebody

Now just in case you think I am far too serious, let me add that I also believe in:

. . . puppies—in all varieties, housebroken and otherwise

. . . barbecued ribs, spicy and dripping with sauce that trickles up to your elbows

. . . paper airplanes that fly for three seconds and hugs that last a lifetime

. . . old pickup trucks that get fifteen miles to the gallon

. . . brand-new Americans, whether they're born that way or speak broken English

. . . and handwritten notes with a scent of lavender, scruffy, ugly fishing hats that should have been thrown away years ago

. . . blooming crocuses that force their way through the ice-capped ground

. . . aging veterans with quivering chins saluting Old Glory

. . . ringing church bells that remind us to take note of what's really important

. . . old photo albums of memories, and roots, and happy days

. . . crisp autumn air, clear-flowing, unbottled water, and the feel of dark, loamy earth and ancient rocks beneath my feet

. . . books that ennoble our thoughts and lessen our intolerance

. . . space launches that connect us with the universe

. . . tsunami relief givers and AIDs workers who connect us with each other

Oh, yes . . . and one thing more. Did I mention that I still believe that on earth, God's work must truly be our own?

Postscript

With so many wonderful truths to explore and others to be discovered, I invite you to join me in collecting more. I have stumbled onto mighty truths in unlikely places. I came upon one from the Grinch, who declared, "Christmas doesn't come from a store." That's worth remembering.

I met a woman recently whose motto was: "Life is too short to dance with ugly people." What an amusing reminder that we should surround ourselves with life-enhancing people. Don't hang out with those who drag you down or make you feel bad.

Yes, powerful affirmations can be a rudder for our lives and an ongoing source of inspiration. I hope that by sharing from my collection of certainties, I have ignited your interest in looking for your own.

If after reading this book, you feel a little more kindly toward a neighbor, coworker, or relative;

. . . if you believe a little harder

. . . if you forgive a little more freely

. . . if you encourage the young, the old, or the hurting more frequently

. . . if you wake up and see each new day as a gift from God packed with possibilities

. . . if you work on what you can give back to your country more than what you can take from it

. . . if a story or quote triggered a smile, a determined effort, or a new way of looking at the world then I am glad to have been a part of your life.

Let me leave you with this final truth: You change the world one person at a time, and the only person you can affect with any certainty is yourself.